C000242847

"For years Rory Noland has mentored thousands ⟨
this new work he takes us to school! Through T
sacred understanding about worship together. E⟨
panied by the generative examples from the first centuries of Christian worship ring in the
reader's ears as we are simultaneously challenged and inspired to rethink the way we conceive
of, craft, and carry out the sacred responsibilities of being a worship leader for today's church.
If you're hoping to find your worship gatherings renewed, this book is for you."

Rod Ellis, worship pastor at Woodburn Baptist Church

"In *Transforming Worship*, Rory Noland makes an excellent case for reenvisioning corporate
worship as a spiritual practice that will actually transform and restore people's souls. His
reenvisioning of worship is historically grounded, deeply thoughtful, and spiritually challenging. I wish that every worship leader in the world would read this vital book!"

Manuel Luz, author of *Honest Worship* and *Imagine That: Discovering Your Unique Role
as a Christian Artist*

"Rory Noland skillfully invites us beyond entertaining worship or informative worship into
what he calls 'transforming worship.' But he's not merely arguing for a new style or brand.
Instead, Rory brings his vast knowledge of church history together with forty-plus years of
church ministry experience to invite us into a robust biblical worship that transforms us from
the inside out. You will learn from the wisdom of many different Christian streams, and more
importantly, discover practical ways to integrate them in your particular context. Rory's
book *Transforming Worship* offers a biblical and historical road map for this constructive,
generative journey that forms us into Christlikeness for the sake of the world."

Aaron Niequist, liturgist and author of *The Eternal Current*

"Rory Noland has studied worship and spiritual formation from the trenches of ministry
for decades. Drawing from culture, Scripture, and scholarship, he balances practical ministry observations with academic rigor and wisely returns us to the foundational components of Christian worship. These insights help us apply practices that endure beyond
worship trends and societal shifts. *Transforming Worship* is a great book to help any worship
leader or pastor in planning worship services and nurturing a worship culture."

John Chilcote, worship professor at Cedarville University

"Rory's thoughts can transform not only the corporate worship you are a part of but your
personal worship as well. Rory's gift for sharing his heart for worship ministry is beautiful
and challenging once again through this book."

Darcy Ruscitti, executive director of central ministries at The Compass Church, Naperville, Illinois

"Having read many of Rory Noland's books on worship, I am convinced *Transforming
Worship* is his most prolific writing to date. It is scholarly, in that he uses an abundance of
authors, theologians, and experts on the subject matter; biblical, in his use of Scripture to
validate his thoughts; spiritual, by supporting the overall essentials of the Christian faith;
and practical, providing examples and suggestions for developing normative worship.
Evangelical churches in America are in desperate need of a worship revival. Rory has outlined every fundamental aspect necessary to accomplish spiritual renewal through a transforming heart of worship."

Terry Williams, president of Priority Worship Ministries

"In a historically young field, Rory has pioneered the importance of the heart's relationship with Jesus in worship and how worship leaders should guide those around them. If you're like me, you crave new tools for growth and development—you will find those tools here. From the beginning of this book all the way to the end, we are given Christ-centered and focused training on a biblical understanding of living out a lifestyle of worship. I highly recommend reading *Transforming Worship* and look forward to sharing it with my teams and leaders!"

David M. Julian, worship pastor at Grace Community Church in Willow Street, Pennsylvania, and the director of the Atoma Worship Conference

"Rory Noland has given Christian worshipers a beautiful gift in helping us to perceive corporate worship as the vital avenue for spiritual transformation. True worship has always been formative; at issue is the degree to which we perceive the liturgy's work within us as a discipling force. This book calls for worship leaders to plan and lead worship in ways that shape worship services to fulfill their formational potential. Noland's many years of both theological reflection on worship and practical experience unite, offering the reader biblical insights and practical implementation."

Constance M. Cherry, professor emeritus of worship and pastoral ministry, Indiana Wesleyan University

"Reading *Transforming Worship* is like enjoying coffee and conversation with a trusted mentor. I can't think of a more reliable guide to the current worship scene than Rory Noland. At a time when some Christian influencers are questioning the need for weekly services, Noland responds with a powerful vision of corporate worship as a gathering of ordinary people encountering an extraordinary God. He brings a generous appreciation of the variety of worship traditions as well as focus and clarity to designing and leading worship services that bring together evangelism and formation rather than forcing them apart. A must-read for pastors and worship leaders."

Robb Redman, professor and director of ministry programs, South College

"Rory is a shepherd, a spiritual father to worship leaders, and my friend. I have witnessed firsthand the unquenchable mission he has to anchor our roots into the Word, respect the rich heritage of God's worshiping people, but without compromising or limiting the unspeakable joy of true spiritual transformation. In plain language, Rory provides for leaders, pastors, and worshipers both a mechanic's manual and a schematic for the vehicle, the road map, and the destination of Christ-centered worship planning—because spiritual formation does matter."

Andi Rozier, Vertical Worship, worship pastor at Harvest Bible Chapel

"Dr. Rory Noland has cleverly taken what would be four years of higher education and made it accessible for every worshiper. From years of practice, experience, and research, Rory has made an excellent modern-day guide to transformative worship experiences. In the hands of the right people, this book could revive our weekly gatherings and be a catalyst for the fulfillment of the Great Commission."

Matthew Thompson, associate professor of worship arts at Hope International University

"Spiritual depth and maturity are critical for fruitfulness and longevity in worship ministry. If you want to move from just leading songs to really pastoring your congregation in spiritually transforming worship, this book is a great place to start."

Matt McCoy, founder of LoopCommunity.com

Transforming
WORSHIP

Planning and Leading
Sunday Services as If Spiritual
Formation Mattered

❧

Rory Noland

Foreword by
Ruth Haley Barton

An imprint of InterVarsity Press
Downers Grove, Illinois

InterVarsity Press
P.O. Box 1400, Downers Grove, IL 60515-1426
ivpress.com
email@ivpress.com

©2021 by Rory Noland

*All rights reserved. No part of this book may be reproduced in any form without written permission
from InterVarsity Press.*

*InterVarsity Press® is the book-publishing division of InterVarsity Christian Fellowship/USA®, a movement of
students and faculty active on campus at hundreds of universities, colleges, and schools of nursing in the United States
of America, and a member movement of the International Fellowship of Evangelical Students. For information about
local and regional activities, visit intervarsity.org.*

*All Scripture quotations, unless otherwise indicated, are taken from The Holy Bible, New International Version®,
NIV®. Copyright © 1973, 1978, 1984, 2011 by Biblica, Inc.™ Used by permission of Zondervan. All rights reserved
worldwide. www.zondervan.com. The "NIV" and "New International Version" are trademarks registered in the
United States Patent and Trademark Office by Biblica, Inc.™*

*While any stories in this book are true, some names and identifying information may have been changed
to protect the privacy of individuals.*

*The publisher cannot verify the accuracy or functionality of website URLs used in this book
beyond the date of publication.*

Cover design and image composite: Cindy Kiple
Interior design: Jeanna Wiggins
Image: abstract red, green, and blue background: © oxygen / Moment Collection / Getty Images

ISBN 978-0-8308-4172-1 (print)
ISBN 978-0-8308-4173-8 (digital)

Printed in the United States of America ∞

*InterVarsity Press is committed to ecological stewardship and to the conservation of natural resources in
all our operations. This book was printed using sustainably sourced paper.*

Library of Congress Cataloging-in-Publication Data
A catalog record for this book is available from the Library of Congress.

P	25	24	23	22	21	20	19	18	17	16	15	14	13	12	11	10	9	8	7	6	5	4	3	2	1
Y	37	36	35	34	33	32	31	30	29	28	27	26	25	24	23	22	21								

Contents

FOREWORD

Ruth Haley Barton

꩜

R ORY AND I GO WAY BACK. We met when we were both on staff
at Willow Creek in the late 90s, early 2000s, but it was on a trip to
Israel with fellow staff members that we first connected meaningfully
around our shared interest in spiritual formation. I was serving as associate director of spiritual formation at the time, and he was serving as
music director, and our first conversations had to do with sharing our
own "longing for more" in the spiritual life as well as a shared desire to
care for the souls of team members engaged in the relentless week in,
week out schedule of producing excellent, culturally relevant church
services and ministries. After we returned home, our conversations continued and even as my journey led me out of that context to found the
Transforming Center and Rory's journey led him to found Heart of the
Artist Ministries, we stayed connected in our search for the more in our
spiritual lives. Eventually Rory joined our two-year *Transforming Community* experience that proved to be the beginning of a fifteen-year
journey of collaboration around transforming worship—one of the
great privileges of my vocational life.

From the Transforming Center's earliest days one of the basic, non-
negotiable elements of our shared practice has been fixed-hour prayer

and worship. The first time a few of us gathered on retreat over twenty years ago, we began with an evening prayer service. We prepared a simple sacred space with a cross, a candle, and an open Bible placed on a simple altar. We entered that space quietly and lit the candle to signify Christ's presence with us through the Holy Spirit. Then, guided by a simple liturgy, we prayed the prayers provided for us beginning with these words:

> *From the rising of the sun to its setting,*
> *Let the name of the Lord be praised.*
>   *YOU, O LORD, ARE MY LAMP.*
>   *MY GOD, YOU MAKE MY DARKNESS BRIGHT.*
> *Light and peace in Jesus Christ our Lord.*
>   *THANKS BE TO GOD.*

We read a Psalm responsively followed by a Psalm prayer that gave us a way to affirm and respond to its message. There was a Gospel reading followed by silence to create space for God to speak to us personally through the chosen Scripture. We prayed some of the oldest prayers of the church—including the Lord's Prayer, written prayers of intercession that helped us offer our shared concerns to God, and spontaneous prayers as well. Some of the prayers were prayed responsively, others in unison, and I remember losing myself in the beauty and simplicity of it all. No bells and whistles needed.

Instead of having to think really, really hard about what to pray, those of us who gathered simply gave ourselves to the beauty and substance of words that expressed deep longings and powerful praises we might never have been able to find words to say. Instead of getting caught in the ego's attempts to say something profound to God (and to the people around us!), we rested from all of that and actually *prayed*. Instead of listening to someone else's interpretation or application of Scripture, the Gospel was read without comment so that we could actually listen for what God was saying personally to us. Rather than being "led" by the up-front gyrations of an overly enthusiastic worship band, there was a sense that we all participated and did it together, having been relieved of the need for a lot of fanfare. After the Scripture reading, this small group of us settled into a silence that was so rich and satisfying that I remember losing all track of time until someone finally nudged me to remind me that it was time to go on!

That simple service lasted all of twenty minutes, and yet we emerged awake and alert to God in the depths of our beings, having given him our whole selves in worship as much as we were able. Even though I had been in church all my life (I am a pastor's kid, after all) it felt like my soul had finally come home to a way of praying and worshiping where there was *space* for a transforming encounter with God in the depths of my being.

That was over twenty years ago now, and we have been praying and worshiping that way ever since—with one notable difference. Until Rory joined us in our second *Transforming Community*, we had not had anyone to lead us in the musical elements of our worship, so our prayer services were made up of words and silence. Even though several of us knew Rory to be an amazing musician, composer, and worship leader we refrained from asking him to serve with these gifts until he had completed his Transforming Community experience. But as soon as he had completed his two-year experience we asked whether he had any vision at all to add some additional worship elements to our fixed-hour prayers.

To our delight, he had already been thinking about this possibility and said yes. And what emerged was a wonderful partnership in which he and I had the opportunity to work together in continuing to develop what we now call Transforming Worship—a way of worshiping that has emerged organically from our life together in community. Partnering with Rory in developing and leading worship services has been one of the most unexpected joys and privileges of my life in ministry.

Over the years as we have planned worship and then reflected on our worship, Rory and I have had countless conversations in which we have attempted to identify characteristics of transforming worship we believe transcend style and can be applied in any worship setting. For us, transforming worship has always been *highly participatory,* leaning into our understanding of the term *liturgy,* which literally means "the work of the people." What a liturgical approach means for us is that our worship is not focused so much on the up-front presence and performance of a few but rather invites everyone to participate in reading and responding to Scripture, to pray and be formed by the prayers of the church, to listen to God in the silent spaces, and to join their voices with others in songs that are simple and yet substantive. In this way we experience transforming worship to be "work" that satisfies and delights us.

We have consistently experienced the truth that transforming worship is *highly experiential,* designed to lead folks into encounters with God that produce some sort of inner shift or change as they respond to that Presence. Transforming prayer and worship is characterized by *simplicity* and includes times of *silence* created specifically for allowing God to speak to us personally and for us to respond. Because we believe transforming worship *engages the whole person,* we are very intentional about incorporating icons, Christian symbols, art, beauty, and guided experiences in our bodies as temples of the Holy Spirit. This is one aspect of bringing all aspects of ourselves into relationship with God in our worship, opening us to a life-transforming encounter. At the same time, we are careful to avoid being emotionally manipulative, overly sentimental or melodramatic—which can be a very fine line to find.

It goes without saying (and yet it needs to be said) that transforming worship is *Christ-centered* in that it creates all sorts of opportunities to open to the transforming presence of Christ together—*in community.* Transforming worship guides us in surrendering—that is, finding ways to offer ourselves as a living sacrifice, holy and acceptable to God, which is our spiritual worship.

In this deeply collaborative journey, God has bestowed significant gifts to us through Rory's leadership. Through his gifts as a composer, God gave us many original compositions written specifically for key moments in our worship services—compositions that to this day help us surrender ourselves to God in very concrete ways so God can do his transforming work. Rory has given us the invaluable experience of being guided by a humble lead worshiper—not a performer drawing attention to himself. Rory has led us, but he has never distracted us. Over and over again young worship leaders have commented about how instructive it has been for them to be led in worship by someone who knew how to call out worship from others rather than drawing attention to himself. And we have benefitted greatly from Rory's teaching and spiritual leadership that is grounded in biblical, theological, and historical reflections on worship—the very grounding you are getting ready to benefit from as you read this work.

And that leads me to my excitement about the book you now have in your hand. I am excited that what we have experienced with Rory as our teacher and worship leader in the Transforming Center is being made available more broadly. I am excited about the intended audience— those who are responsible for making Sunday services happen. What a sacred privilege and responsibility this is and one that should be approached with serious preparation and intentionality. I am excited that Rory casts a clear vision for transforming worship as a vital spiritual discipline that can move us beyond nominal Christianity. I am stirred by his unpacking of the biblical, theological, and historical underpinnings of transforming worship that locate this conversation in the context of historic Christianity and not just the last three hundred years. I am thrilled with how practical this book is in offering real, workable ideas for incorporating historic Christian practices into our worship services—practices that have been tested by time and have proven themselves to open us to God's transforming work as we come together. And I just love the Checklist for Transforming Worship Services Rory includes as an appendix.

Most of all, I am thrilled with the questions this book will raise for you and your team:

- What is transforming worship?

- What would it look like to plan worship services as if spiritual transformation matters and we are seeking it as a real outcome?

- How can transforming worship play a pivotal role in stemming the tide of nominal Christianity in our church?

- What are the biblical origins of transforming worship and what does that mean to us in our setting?

- Who should be the priority on Sunday morning—believers or unbelievers?

- How should Protestants view sacred symbols and sacramental rituals?

- What are the significant elements of a transforming worship service? How is such a service put together?

If these questions excite you as much as they excite me, you are in for a treat! And not just a treat but a substantive meal that will nourish you as you set the table for others.

There is a famous quote from Rainer Marie Rilke's *Letters to a Young Poet* in which he says "Be patient toward all that is unsolved in your heart. Try to love the questions themselves, like locked rooms and like books that are written in a very foreign tongue." The questions above are questions to love and to nurture as we refuse to give in to the seduction of easy answers and forced solutions brought too quickly and before their time. Instead, I pray there is a group of you that can be patient and take time to live with these questions, seeing how God might use them to lead you. I believe that if pastors and elders, worship leaders and teams engage this book together and begin incorporating even a fraction of the wealth contained here, your worship experience will be changed and your people will be changed. Transformed, even! May it be so.

INTRODUCTION

What Is Transforming Worship?

❦

I HAVE A CONFESSION TO MAKE: I am directionally challenged. My wife can go somewhere and years later drive to the exact location. I, on the other hand, couldn't find the place if I had been there the day before. When we're driving through the suburbs of Chicago and my lovely wife instructs me to "turn south," I gently remind her that if I knew which way Canada was, I'd head in the opposite direction. But since I haven't a clue, a simple imperative—turn left or right—prevents us from ending up in Lake Michigan. I am indebted to whoever invented the GPS for getting me to more appointments on time than I deserve.

Think of this book as a GPS for those who plan and lead worship services. Our destination is church—specifically, a vision for church services that I'm calling *transforming worship*. My two biggest passions are worship and spiritual formation. I've often wondered, *What would it look like to conceive of gathered worship as if spiritual formation mattered? How would that affect the way we plan and lead worship services?* In Romans 12:1-2, Paul explains that as we worship our minds are constantly being renewed. By juxtaposing worship and transformation Paul establishes a fundamental link between the two. This book explores the dynamic interplay between worship and spiritual formation and imagines what it would be like to approach Sunday services with greater intentionality toward transformation.

For the last fifteen years I've had the privilege of leading worship for the Transforming Center, a retreat ministry that specializes in spiritual formation for leaders. Participants gather quarterly to experience substantive teaching on themes and practices related to spiritual formation. The Transforming Center represents a growing movement of pastors and leaders who are realigning their church's priorities around discipleship.

Scripture emphasizes that spiritual formation is the foundational task of the church. Jesus charged his followers to make disciples, baptize them, and teach them to live in obedience to his commands (Matthew 28:19-20). The Great Commission is fundamentally a call to produce disciples—obedient followers—of Jesus Christ who in turn make other disciples. In John 17, on the eve of his crucifixion, Jesus prays what many believe to be the deepest desires of his heart, including an urgent prayer that his followers be sanctified (John 17:17).

New Testament church leaders had no confusion about their overarching mission. Paul was adamant that God wants every believer to be sanctified (1 Thessalonians 4:3), so he aspired to bring his people to full maturity in Christ (Colossians 1:28). His goal was not merely to win a lot of people to Christ but to help them mature spiritually and to equip them for ministry in the community at large (Ephesians 4:12). Paul took his calling to make disciples so seriously that he agonized over the spiritual well-being of his people; he longed for them to experience genuine transformation and for Christ to be truly formed in them (Galatians 4:19). The apostle and his colleagues in Colossae prayed fervently that their flock would be filled with knowledge, wisdom, and understanding to live worthy of and pleasing to the Lord (Colossians 1:9-10). Paul was constantly on his knees praying that his people would reap all the spiritual benefits of knowing Christ (Ephesians 1:17-19), that they would be sanctified "through and through" (1 Thessalonians 5:23). The writer of Hebrews beseeched the Lord to work in the lives of his people to equip them to do God's will (Hebrews 13:21).

Scripture indicates that the church's main agenda is to train believers to walk, empowered by grace, in the freedom of Christ. Making disciples is not a sidebar activity relegated to a specialized subministry of the church; it is not the pet project of the church's education department or the latest trend the church rallies around for a few months but abandons when the next popular craze comes along. Spiritual formation is not an optional pursuit but the very reason the church exists in the first place. For that reason church leaders are responsible for providing their flocks with resources and opportunities to help them grow spiritually. Transforming worship views Sunday morning as a golden opportunity to nurture the spiritual lives of God's people.

Defining Transforming Worship

I define *transforming worship* as "a communal experience that combines classic spiritual practices with a formative encounter with God in Christ through the Holy Spirit." Notice, first, that it's communal; it is something we do in the company of others, in partnership with God's people. It is also experiential; the bulk of the activities are not designed for people to sit back and watch but to join in and participate. Transforming worship draws from traditional Christian disciplines such as prayer, Scripture reading, confession, the Lord's Supper, and baptism, all of which the church has been practicing since its inception. The assumption here is that every major part of the service, not just the sermon, can be spiritually formative. At the heart of this entire experience is an encounter with the Lord Jesus Christ. Transforming worship does not seek to evoke a feeling or deliver teaching but to encounter a person. The ultimate goal is for worshipers to encounter the life-altering, character-shaping presence of God.

Allen Ross offers a compelling vision for worship that takes seriously its inherent potential to transform lives:

> For worship to be as glorious as it should be, for it to lift people out of their mundane cares and fill them with adoration and praise, for it to be the life-changing and life-defining experience it was designed to be, it must be inspired by a vision so great and so glorious that what we call worship will be transformed from a routine gathering into a transcendent meeting with the living God.

Ross's glorious vision of worship hinges not on the quality of our praise music but our attentiveness to the formative nature of Sunday services.

THOU SHALL NOT MESS WITH WORSHIP!

I am well aware that any talk about making adjustments to Sunday services makes church leaders nervous. One pastor told me that he was willing to hire a different worship leader and raise thousands of dollars for a new sound system but that he wouldn't dream of introducing changes to the actual service. "Mess with Sunday morning at your own risk!" he sternly warned, as if brandishing an eleventh commandment. His foreboding admonishment was gleaned from painful experience. I completely understand such apprehension. I've seen enough worship wars during my lifetime to heighten my trepidation about tampering with the service. My fears are allayed, however, by the fact that transforming worship has nothing to do with a certain style of music or method of worship. Nor am I promoting a particular genre of musical praise. I'm not saying that music and methodology are not important, but those are peripheral, ephemeral issues, not substantive ones. Worship styles change, music evolves, but biblical precepts regarding worship do not change with the times. The principles in this book, therefore, apply to all churches—mainline, nondenominational, independent, charismatic, liturgical, spontaneous, traditional, or contemporary. Instead of advancing a new, trend-setting philosophy of worship, I'm appealing to the modern church to return to a biblical vision of gathered worship as a formative spiritual practice.

After learning what the Bible says about worship, some churches might decide to make sweeping changes to their services. In those cases I trust that leaders will explain the rationale for those changes based on biblical precedence rather than some innovative initiative about church growth or cultural relevancy. However, after reading this book I believe most churches will make significant but more subtle, incremental changes. That's because the main elements of a transforming worship service are already in place at every church but need to be emphasized or treated not as slots to fill in a worship order but as potentially formative elements. As we shall see, activities that Christians have been doing together since the beginning—things like prayer and Bible reading—were originally designed for the purpose of edification. Approaching these activities as well as the entire service more mindful of spiritual formation will inevitably produce changes. However, those changes will benefit all involved. Achieving a transforming worship service, therefore, need not be a painful experience for leaders or laypeople. In the long run, congregation members will discover that a more formative approach to worship enhances their Sunday morning experience.

TODAY'S URGENCY

There is an urgent need today for church services that are more spiritually substantive. In recent decades the church has failed to make spiritual formation a priority, and the results have been devastating. The church is to be commended for making outreach and evangelism high priorities, but we have done a poor job of discipling and assimilating new believers into the life of the church. Gregory Jones laments that today's church leaders and their congregations have been so inadequately formed in their faith that they cannot live the Christian life in all its fullness. Jones further observes that those who join mainline Protestant churches these days are not required to make any changes to the way they live; neither are they given the resources to implement such changes. The church's inattentiveness to spiritual formation has too often resulted in nominal Christians who experienced a spiritual awakening when they came to the Lord (and perhaps a certain degree of life change), but they are no longer on the journey toward radical transformation in Christ.

I believe that transforming worship can play a pivotal role in stemming the tide of nominal Christianity. The urgency of the situation demands that our church services take on a more spiritually formative role. In other words it's time to mess with the service to bring it in line with its original design as a spiritually formative practice.

Transforming Worship is geared to all those responsible for making Sunday services happen: pastors, worship leaders, volunteers, and lay leaders. The book is divided into two parts; the first half examines transforming worship conceptually from a biblical, historical, and theological perspective. The second section presents five communal spiritual practices intrinsic to a transforming worship experience: prayer, Scripture reading, confession, the Lord's Supper, and baptism. Each chapter of the book ends with practical suggestions on how to implement the material that's presented in your particular setting. I hope this book encourages you, rejuvenates you, and proves helpful as you seek a more formative approach to Sunday services. May the Lord bless you as you continue to faithfully serve those you lead every week in worship.

Part 1

BIBLICAL, HISTORICAL, AND THEOLOGICAL FOUNDATIONS OF TRANSFORMING WORSHIP

꒰ꙮ꒱

TRANSFORMING WORSHIP is not a new idea; it has biblical and historical precedence and is grounded in a sound theology of worship. In these opening chapters we'll first investigate the biblical origins of transforming worship and glean principles that both the Old and New Testaments endorse. We will then identify a working template, again drawn from Scripture, that is not intended to be a rigid order of service but a general outline or shape for corporate worship. Chapter three showcases a New Testament model for transforming worship that clarifies who should be more of a priority on Sunday morning: believers or unbelievers. In my research for this book I kept looking for the best example of a church that conducted worship as if spiritual formation mattered. I eventually landed on the early church. So for a historical perspective, chapter four examines how those early Christians incorporated the biblical principles of worship into their Sunday services.

Chapter five focuses on a theology of the sacred and seeks to answer important questions about sacramentality. How should Protestants view sacred symbols and religious rituals? Is there a philosophy of the sacred—of sacramentality—that is appropriate for the twenty-first century? What do symbology, ritual, and sacramentality have to do with modern worship? The biblical, historical, and theological perspectives not only provide a firm foundation for transforming worship, but they also enhance our vision of what it looks like and entails.

1

IT ALL STARTED AT SINAI

❦

FOR THE LAST SEVERAL YEARS I have served as a consultant for churches seeking to improve the overall worship experience at their Sunday services. Though situations vary, churches typically bring me in to help them get from point A to point B. I put it that way because I've found that church leaders always have an idea of what point B looks like. In other words, they have a vision, an idea of what they want to see happen every Sunday at their church. If I've learned one thing from my experience doing church work, it's that everyone has a picture in their mind of what constitutes real or true worship. Some of our preconceived notions of worship are based on the church we grew up in or one we previously attended. We're comfortable with a certain style of worship simply because we're used to it; it's familiar to us. Some are attracted to a particular type of music; they can't engage unless the music is "right." Others have a notion of worship derived from a megachurch they visited or a conference they attended that featured a professional quality worship band.

I can't help but notice that most everyone's concept of worship, including my own, mirrors our personal experience and preferences. But what about God? What does God think about worship? We assume that if the worship feels right to us, it must feel right to God, which is presumptuous. How do we know for sure how God feels about our particular brand of worship? Does God have a favorite style of music? Is the style of music even important to God?

Fortunately, God has revealed in his Word how he desires to be worshiped, and, surprisingly, it has little if anything to do with music. Exodus 1–15 presents the story of God rescuing the Israelites from slavery in Egypt. This epic drama culminated in a meeting between God and his chosen people at Mount Sinai, during which God prescribed how he desires to be worshiped. In this chapter we will explore the foundational principles of corporate worship gleaned from Israel's encounter with God atop Mount Sinai and assess how to apply those principles to modern worship.

Sinai School of Worship

As recorded in Exodus 3, Moses was tending sheep at Mount Sinai when God spoke to him through a burning bush and revealed his plan to rescue Israel from slavery. God promised Moses that after delivering his people he would bring them to the very spot where Moses was standing, specifically so they could worship God (Exodus 3:12; 7:16).

We assume that if the worship feels right to us, it must feel right to God, which is presumptuous.

Fast forward several years to the same location. God has led Israel out of Egypt and directed them to Mount Sinai, just as he promised (Exodus 19–32). Freed from the shackles of slavery, the people were now free to worship. But before they could do so, God established his covenant with them and offered instructions concerning how he wants to be worshiped. After all, Israel had been entrenched in a pagan society for over four hundred years; judging from their actions in the desert, they no longer consistently reflected the piety of their faith tradition. For example, their constant complaining throughout their sojourn demonstrated a blatant lack of trust in God, especially in light of all the miracles he performed to rescue them. The moaning and griping were pervasive; Scripture notes the frequency with which the entire community grumbled against Moses and Aaron (Exodus 16:2, 8; 17:2-4, 7). The most disgruntled among them longed for the comforts of Egypt even if it meant returning to slavery (Exodus 14:11-12; 16:3), which discloses an ignorance of their true identity. They were a nation destined for greatness, who, according to the Abrahamic covenant, would eventually bless all the peoples of the earth (Genesis 12:1-3; 15:1-5; 17:1-8).

The Exodus account contains no indication that the people worshiped together during their six-week sojourn to Sinai. Except for a brief praise song they sang on the shores of the Red Sea (Exodus 15), the narrative mentions no regular worship observances. Apparently, gathered worship did not play a vital role in the ongoing life of the community. The Israelites had been subjected to the prevailing Egyptian culture for so long they had formed an incomplete concept of God, lost their identity as God's chosen, covenant people, and had no established routine for gathered worship.

At Mount Sinai, God was now calling these former slaves to be his treasured possession, a kingdom of priests, and a holy nation (Exodus 19:5-6). In other words God was inviting them to be his specially chosen people and to partner with him in his global mission to redeem his fallen creation. God brought Israel to Sinai for what Samuel Balentine portrays as a sabbath experience—a furlough that began during the seventh week of the exodus, which lasted for eleven months (Numbers 10:11), and afforded the Israelites an extended time of deliberation to reflect on the implications of their covenant relationship with God. Because the concept of covenant plays a vital role in worship theology, a brief analysis of a typical Old Testament covenant is in order.

Covenants in antiquity. In the ancient world a covenant was a treaty or agreement between two parties; typically one party was superior to the other. For example, a powerful king, nation, or tribe would enter into an official agreement with a weaker one. The stronger ruler was often referred to as "lord," the weaker one as "servant." The terms of the covenant bound the lord to protect the servant who in turn pledged unwavering allegiance to the lord, which meant going to war against the lord's enemies as well as paying tribute to his authority. Alliances formed by a covenant, therefore, were politically and socially motivated.

A covenant transaction adhered to a standard protocol that began with a brief narrative chronicling the participants' shared history. Terms of the agreement were then spelled out, the benefits, obligations, and responsibilities for both parties were clearly indicated. Punitive measures for treaty violations were also detailed. A physical sign, such as a scar, was often used to seal the agreement, and the lesser king or nation would be given a new name indicating that they were now owned, in a sense, by their new leader. Finally, the covenant was captured and preserved in a document that served to remind both parties of their pact.

Covenants in antiquity were typically ratified in a special ceremony that incorporated some type of blood sacrifice. Participants were either sprinkled with the blood of a sacrificial animal or they would walk between pieces of the animal that had been cut up for the occasion, a ritual that communicated "May the gods cut me to pieces, should I violate the terms of this treaty." Covenant partners sometimes shared a meal to ratify the pact. Although God also entered into covenants with Noah (Genesis 9:1-17), Abraham (Genesis 12:2-3; 15; 17:1-22), and David (2 Samuel 7:11-16), it was the agreement God initiated with Moses that profoundly influenced Israel's approach to worship.

Sinai worship service. The ratification of the Mosaic covenant, recorded in Exodus 24, occurred in the context of a worship service. God, always the initiator in the human-divine relationship, summoned Moses so the Lord and he could meet before Moses met with the people (Exodus 24:1). Then Moses called the Israelites together and, following

God's previous orders (Exodus 21–23), began to share with them all the words that God spoke to him atop Mount Sinai (Exodus 24:3). What the text summarizes in one verse comprises four chapters of the book of Exodus (20–23). In what must have been a lengthy sermon, Moses taught the Ten Commandments (Exodus 20:1-17) and presented the terms of Israel's covenant agreement with God, known subsequently as the Book of the Covenant (Exodus 20:22–23:33). Interestingly, the Book of the Covenant begins and ends with explicit instructions about worship: Exodus 20:22-26 calls for God's faithful to offer sacrifices on an altar; Exodus 23:10-12 commands them to observe weekly Sabbath. This passage also includes three festivals that God instructed them to observe annually—Passover, the Festival of Harvest, and the Festival of Ingathering (Exodus 23:14-19). Upon hearing God's instructions the congregation responded by vowing to obey God's laws (Exodus 24:3). The Sinai sermon, therefore, was substantive, was received as the word of God for his people, and elicited a response from them as well.

When Moses finished delivering God's word, he built an altar and offered sacrifices, both of which were activities God previously instructed him to do (Exodus 24:4-5). As part of the sacrificial ritual, Moses sprinkled the people with blood from the sacrificial oxen (Exodus 24:8), which, following ancient custom, bound covenant partners together in mutual loyalty. Therefore, Israel's ritual of animal sacrifice, the centerpiece of Old Testament worship, was inaugurated at Mount Sinai as an expression of their loyalty and commitment to God. The ceremony climaxed with Moses leading Israel's seventy elders up Mount Sinai to commune with God as God had earlier prescribed (Exodus 24:1, 9-11). Atop Sinai, Israel's leaders "saw God, and they ate and drank" (Exodus 24:11). They encountered God and shared a meal in his presence. Though Israel emerged from slavery as a ragtag tribe without a cogent religious identity and with no compelling vision for worship, they left Sinai for the Promised Land as what Balentine characterizes as both a covenant community as well as a worshiping community. Indeed, God had personally schooled them regarding who he is, who they were, and how God desires to be worshiped.

IMPLICATIONS OF THE WORSHIP AT SINAI
FOR SUNDAY SERVICES TODAY

Robbie Castleman maintains that the Israelite's unique approach to worship distinguished them from all neighboring tribes and nations. Let's examine these distinctive features of worship derived from the exodus story and consider their implications for transforming worship gatherings. The foundational principles listed in this and the following chapter draw extensively from Constance Cherry's book *The Worship Architect: A Blueprint for Designing Culturally Relevant and Biblically Faithful Services.*

God-initiated meeting between God and his people. Sinai reveals that God is the one who initiates worship. God is the one who summoned Moses for a mountaintop meeting and then charged him with the responsibility of facilitating the larger gathering between God and his people. God also dictated the vital terms of the gathering. Instead of leaving the details entirely up to Moses, God determined the time, the place, and what everyone was to do when they gathered. Biblical worship is never on our terms—never about us and our personal preferences—but wholly on God's terms.

The fact that God initiates worship completely changes the dynamics of a church service. On Sundays we're not simply attending a church service; we're going, by divine invitation, to meet with God and his people. Gathered worship is more than a teaching time, more than a Christian sing-along; it is a divine invitation to encounter and experience God. Like the Israelites, we too have to carve time out of our schedules to enter into a Sabbath experience. As our Jewish ancestors made the arduous trek to Sinai, we too must exert the energy to travel to a specific place—our local church—to experience God's presence among his people. All that we do during worship is in response to the divine presence, to God's self-revelation. Jesus taught that our heavenly Father is constantly looking for people ready and willing to meet with him (John 4:23-24). Sunday worship is fundamentally a meeting between God and his people, initiated by God himself. Every time we gather, we take God up on his holy invitation to come together with our brothers and sisters in Christ to fellowship with God.

Dialogical nature of worship. Moses shared with the people all that God revealed to him, and they responded. Gathered worship is essentially a dialogue between God and his people. God speaks, we listen and respond; we speak and God hears us, and he too responds. God reveals himself mainly through his Word; we respond verbally by singing or with actions. Constance Cherry emphasizes that while some methods for planning worship result in God being the topic of conversation, approaching worship as a dialogue enables God to be a partner in the conversation. Gathered worship is an encounter with a God who is an active conversationalist.

Healthy and constructive dialogue is never one-sided; it is not a monologue. Both parties actively participate in the conversation. To achieve this sense of dialogue in a group setting requires participation on the part of all involved. Biblical worship does not entail watching someone else converse with God or passively listening to a sermon; it requires all worshipers to take part in this dynamic dialogue with God. The fact that true worship is dialogical means that on any given Sunday God could say something significant and meaningful to us during the service.

Proclaiming who God is and what God has done. After God parted the Red Sea and the children of Israel crossed safely to the other side, Moses led the people in a spontaneous praise song. The Song of Moses, found in Exodus 15, is one of the first—if not the first—worship songs recorded in the Bible. This ancient praise song is about God and is sung to God. The lyrics are celebrative and triumphant, focusing on who God is and what God accomplished in delivering Israel.

In the first three verses God is exalted as "Lord," "my strength," "my defense," "my salvation," "my God," and "a warrior." Moses' song celebrates who God is by highlighting some of his attributes. Verses 4-5 go on to describe how God hurled Pharaoh's army into the water and subdued them. Linking God's actions to his attributes underscores that God's deeds flow out of who he is. The rest of Moses' song goes back and forth between describing who God is and citing what God did to rescue Israel.

The Song of Moses illustrates that a fundamental task for gathered worshipers is to proclaim who God is and celebrate God's marvelous deeds of deliverance. David too purposed to speak of the "glorious splendor" of God and to meditate on God's "wonderful works" (Psalm 145:5). And according to Scripture, the main reason Christians gather is to declare the praises of him who called us "out of darkness into his wonderful light" (1 Peter 2:9). Proclaiming who God is and celebrating all that God has done instills hope as we anticipate all that God is yet to do.

Focusing on God's character and his actions also increases our appreciation for his incomparability. Midway through the Song of Moses the singers exclaim,

> Who among the gods
>   is like you, LORD?
> Who is like you—
>   majestic in holiness,
> awesome in glory,
>   working wonders? (Exodus 15:11)

God's attributes and wondrous deeds prove that there is absolutely no one like our God; no one does the things he does. Extoling the Lord and his mighty deeds keeps our worship centered on our great, incomparable, transcendent God.

Expression of our covenant relationship with God. The Sinai worship experience allowed Israel to ratify its covenant agreement with God. The

essence of a covenant, as you recall, is that it establishes a
relationship between two parties and clarifies their
obligations and responsibilities toward each other.
Through the Mosaic covenant, God made a
commitment to relate to Israel as his chosen
people; they would be the recipients of his
steadfast, loyal love (Exodus 20:6). To uphold
their end of the agreement, the Israelites were
asked to remain loyal to God and his ways. Thus,
after Moses read the Book of the Covenant, the
people responded, "We will do everything the
LORD has said; we will obey" (Exodus 24:7). To
remain in good standing with God, the people

> *Extoling
> the Lord and
> his mighty
> deeds keeps our
> worship centered
> on our great,
> incomparable,
> transcendent
> God.*

of Israel were expected to live lives of godly obedience and moral integrity. Israel's worship, notes Castleman, was designed to be an
expression of their unique identity as God's covenant people.

Christians, of course, live under the new covenant written in the
blood of Christ (Luke 22:20). Israel consistently failed to live up to the
terms of the Mosaic covenant, so God, speaking through the prophet
Jeremiah, promised to provide a new arrangement, which he would
write on the hearts of his people (Jeremiah 31:31-33). The early church
quickly realized that God had enacted this new covenant through
Christ, for Jesus is the only one who truly fulfills God's requirements
for holiness and obedience. Jesus did not come to revoke the concept
of covenant but to fulfill it on our behalf. By offering himself as the
unblemished, sacrificial lamb (Hebrews 9:28; 1 Peter 1:19), Jesus takes
on our covenant obligations—the ones neither Israel nor anyone else
has ever been able to meet—and keeps the covenant in our stead.
Under the new covenant God demonstrates his love, mercy, and grace
through Jesus, whose blood was poured out for the forgiveness of sin
(Matthew 26:28).

Worship is an expression of our covenant relationship with God. In the same way that Israel's worship affirmed their identity as God's people, Sunday worship defines Christians as people of God's new covenant written in the blood of Christ. Transforming worship encourages God's people to remain faithful to our commitment to follow Christ and helps us grow in our relationship with the Lord.

Reenacting God's saving acts of redemption. Israel's worship practices went beyond declaring God's deeds of deliverance and actually involved a vivid reenactment of them. Israel's worship practices revolved around remembering that God rescued them from bondage and then reenacting or re-presenting that deliverance. At Sinai, God prescribed a set of rituals and festivals for his people to observe as an expression of their covenant relationship with him. Each sacred act incorporated specific symbols combined with well-orchestrated actions and gestures to help Israel recall, relive, and commemorate God's redemptive, historical work in the world. God instituted Passover, for example, as a permanent feast designed to help his chosen people relive and commemorate the Hebrew slaves' last night of bondage in Egypt.

Transforming worship encourages God's people to remain faithful to our commitment to follow Christ and helps us grow in our relationship with the Lord.

Like Passover, the Lord's Supper also uses symbolism and gestures to help Christians relive the death and resurrection of Jesus Christ. (Chapter five delves more deeply into the role that symbols and sacred acts play in spiritual formation; chapter nine details the spiritual implications of the Lord's Supper. For now, suffice it to say that symbols and sacred gestures are a means God has provided to help us reenact his story of redemption and deliverance during worship.)

GUIDING PRINCIPLES FOR TRANSFORMING WORSHIP

Israel's experience at Sinai discloses God's perspective on worship—
that it is a meeting of God's people with God that God himself initiates
and that the gathering is dialogical. Furthermore, every time we assemble, we have the privilege of proclaiming to each other and to the
world who God is and all God has done. Public worship also allows us
to renew our commitment to the Lord and to reenact—relive—God's
cosmic story of deliverance.

Sinai's worship principles proved to be transformative. Our
Hebrew ancestors heard God's word—the Ten Commandments and
the rules of the covenant—which challenged them to live a different
kind of life in allegiance to God and his ways. God's people offered
burned sacrifices as evidence of their desire to follow the Lord. They
also verbally expressed their intentions to obey. The purpose of
worship is not spiritual formation per se, but that is the natural result
of experiencing God. From its inception worship was designed to be
a spiritually formative encounter with the Lord. For that reason, the
guidelines God laid down at Sinai are foundational to a transforming
worship service.

HOW ARE THE BIBLICAL PRINCIPLES OF
WORSHIP MANIFESTED IN YOUR SETTING?

For those seeking a more formative approach to planning and leading
worship, the five principles gleaned from Exodus give ample reason to
pause and consider how to apply these concepts to our particular settings.

1. *God-initiated meeting between God and his people.* Do the people
   we lead sense that we are meeting with God when we gather on
   Sunday? Or are they coming to church merely to hear the pastor
   preach? Are there any prayers, songs, or Scripture readings we
   can incorporate to underscore that God is the one calling us
   to gather?

2. *Dialogical nature of worship.* How can we help the congregation understand and experience the verticality of worship? Are we giving them enough opportunities to speak to God? If so, how can we help them engage like they're speaking to God? What does it look like in our setting to give worshipers opportunities for God to speak to them? Could brief moments of silence or reflection help them hear from the Lord? How can we help congregation members personalize and apply what God is saying to them through his word?

3. *Proclaiming who God is and what God has done.* Do our services do an adequate job of proclaiming who God is and celebrating all that God has done and continues to do in the world? Though it's meaningful and appropriate to sing personal songs expressing love and devotion to God, do the lyrics we sing ever get out of balance and focus more on us than on the Lord? Do we present the full range of God's attributes over time, or do we keep emphasizing our favorites?

4. *Expression of our covenant relationship with God.* Do our services inspire worshipers to follow Christ? Do we call our people to faithful obedience to biblical Christianity? Do we invite believers into deeper intimacy with the Lord? How can we allow our people to express or renew their commitment to God?

5. *Reenacting God's saving acts of redemption.* How can we ensure that how we observe the Lord's Supper and baptism is spiritually formative? What are the spiritual implications of these sacred acts that we need to emphasize more? What can we do to help our people encounter Jesus in the Lord's Supper?

At Mount Sinai the Israelites learned how to worship God, and they became a nation of worshipers. I hope that churches today will apply the principles God revealed to our Hebrew brothers and sisters and discover what it truly means to be a worshiping community.

2

UPDATING THE ANCIENT FORMULA
FOR SUNDAY SERVICES

❦

I N RECENT YEARS I've been conducting an informal survey of worship leaders asking them to describe their approach to planning services. "What is your philosophy of worship," I typically ask, "and how does it drive the way you plan and lead Sunday services?" The answers I receive differ greatly from one another. Some worship planners take the fast-to-slow route, for example; they start with several upbeat tunes but eventually wind down to a couple of slow songs at the end. One leader told me that, for musical convenience, she strings together songs that are in the same key. Some point to a single Scripture passage as the basis for their entire philosophy of worship. John 4:23-24—worshipping in Spirit and truth—constitutes true worship in some circles. Some congregations model their services on Isaiah 6. Others try to replicate the experience of the Old Testament Jews as they journeyed to the temple for worship. Still others follow a tradition or the prescribed methods of their denomination.

On one hand, the various approaches have resulted in a rich diversity of worship experiences. People today have access to a wide variety of worship styles, a wealth of creative and artistic expressions of worship. After all, no one style of worship completely captures the fullness of our God. On the other hand, all that wonderful freedom and diversity raises questions. Should we all follow at least some basic format or general design? Is there a framework or structure that allows for diversity but keeps us all on the same page? If so, what does that structure look like?

The Bible does not contain a detailed order of service for worship; there is no sanctified set list to emulate. Historians report that the early church witnessed a great deal of variety in the way Christians conducted worship. Within this diversity the biblical narrative and the historical record both suggest a basic shape or framework for worship in the early church, the inspiration for which derived from the Emmaus story in the Gospel of Luke. Emmaus's greatest contribution to worship is the template it provides for a transformative approach to Sunday services.

> *The early church witnessed a great deal of variety in the way Christians conducted worship.*

THE EMMAUS ENCOUNTER

The Emmaus narrative confirms all the significant truths gleaned from the exodus story that were discussed in chapter one. Atop Mount Sinai, God the Father took the first step in the relationship with Israel and initiated the proceedings. On the Emmaus road, God the Son initiated a conversation with a pair of road-weary companions; he simply approached them and asked what they were discussing (Luke 24:15-17). Jesus drew them into a conversation, which confirms what Israel learned at Sinai—that gathered worship is a divinely initiated meeting that is dialogical.

In the same way that Moses shared God's word with the people, Jesus explained to Cleopas and his unnamed friend all that the Scriptures said about himself (Luke 24:27). The two disciples felt like their hearts were on fire as they listened to Jesus' teaching (Luke 24:32). They returned to Jerusalem later that evening proclaiming that Jesus is Lord and that he rose from the dead (Luke 24:34-35), supporting the Old Testament's assertion that worship proclaims who God is and what God has done.

Since Jesus' teaching drew extensively on Moses and the prophets, he undoubtedly explained to his Emmaus friends how his death and resurrection fulfilled the Mosaic covenant and confirmed that he is the author of Jeremiah's new covenant. By reframing their concept of the covenant, Jesus implicitly invited them to commit to following him.

The Emmaus story climaxes with Jesus re-creating the scene in the upper room, where he shared a Passover meal with his followers the night before he was crucified. Sitting around a small, intimate table set for three, Jesus broke bread with his companions, prompting them to finally recognize him as their crucified but now risen Savior (Luke 24:30-31). The Emmaus experience furthers the precedent Sinai set for gathered worship to reenact God's saving acts of redemption.

In addition to affirming all of Sinai's salient features regarding worship, Emmaus discloses another characteristic exclusive to Christian worship—that it is Christocentric. After their heart-stirring encounter with the risen Christ, Cleopas and his friend scurried off to Jerusalem proclaiming that Jesus is Lord (Luke 24:34).

The apostle John's eyewitness account of heavenly worship includes a breathtaking scene in which the four living creatures and twenty-four elders fall before the Lamb of God, thousands of angels raise loud voices, and all creation ascribes praise, honor, glory, and power to Jesus Christ forever and ever (Revelation 5:8-13). That which sets Christianity apart from all other religions is its worship of Jesus as Lord and Savior.

As the church developed the concept of the Trinity, it added one more principle to its theology of worship. Early theologians established that Christian worship is distinctly trinitarian, meaning three things:

1. We pray to the Father, through the Son, in the Spirit (i.e., "in the name of the Father, the Son, and the Holy Spirit").

2. We pray to each of the three persons of the Trinity.

3. We glorify God the Father, God the Son, and God the Holy Spirit.

Even though it took the church almost four hundred years to formulate an official theology of the Trinity, extant documents reveal that its earliest liturgies, prayers, baptisms, and Communion services employed trinitarian language. From the beginning, Christian worship has always been by nature trinitarian.

> *From the beginning, Christian worship has always been by nature trinitarian.*

Finally, the Emmaus account is a microcosm of a believer's journey to spiritual transformation. The two companions were lost, confused, downcast, and without hope. Jesus sought them out, revealed himself to them, and helped them see and understand the truth. Their eyes were opened, their hearts were stirred, and they were forever changed. The two disciples encountered the living Christ and were transformed by his presence among them.

THE EMMAUS TEMPLATE FOR GATHERED WORSHIP

The Emmaus encounter became instrumental in shaping Christian worship by providing a pattern for Sunday services. Robert Webber is among the many scholars who detected a progression of four movements in the Emmaus account that is consistent with divine-human encounters throughout Scripture. Constance Cherry effectively links the fourfold sequence to Luke's narrative. The basic contour of the Emmaus encounter suggests four sequential components for worship services: gathering, Word, Table, and sending (see fig. 2.1).

GATHERING → WORD → TABLE → SENDING

Figure 2.1. Historic fourfold order of service

This progression effectively captures what Cleopas and his friend experienced in their encounter with Christ. Jesus drew the Emmaus pilgrims into a conversation; he gathered the three of them together. He shared the Word of God and explained its meaning. Then, sitting at the table together, Jesus made himself known to them in the breaking of bread. Their life-changing encounter with the risen Savior sent the comrades from Emmaus back into the world—to Jerusalem—to proclaim that Jesus Christ had risen from the dead, that he was truly alive. The fourfold progression permeating the Emmaus adventure constitutes a biblical approach to planning and leading corporate worship.

Historians observe that even though methods varied from one location to another, the four movements outlined in figure 2.1 emerged early as a common structure among Christian gatherings. At first, a twofold worship order of Word and Table was standard practice. As chronicled in Acts 2:42, the New Testament church was devoted to the apostles' teaching and to the breaking of bread, among other things. The earliest believers, most of whom were Jews, continued their lifelong practice of meeting at the synagogue, where they would read selections from their Hebrew Bible and listen as someone commented on them. History's first Jews for Jesus interpreted those Scriptures in light of their belief that Christ is the Messiah. They also broke bread together daily (Acts 2:46). Following the Emmaus model in which Jesus was made known in the Scriptures and in the breaking of bread, God's Word and Communion quickly gained prominence as foundational elements for Christian worship. Two additional components, gathering and sending, were soon added as bookends to Word and Table. By the third century the fourfold worship service had become the norm for the Christian church and is still strictly followed by traditional, liturgical churches. However, an increasing number of non-liturgical churches are now adopting this format for their services. The function of each segment of the sequence reflects its vital contribution to worship as a spiritually formative experience for God's people.

The *gathering* brings the community together around the unique manifestation of God's presence that is gathered worship. Lasting anywhere from ten to thirty minutes, the gathering can include a variety of elements such as praise songs, hymns, prayer, readings, Scripture, and video. Some traditions also include a time of confession during the gathering. This opening portion typically begins with a call to worship that is either spoken or sung. An effective call to worship establishes that God is the one calling us together. Humans may sing or pronounce the call, the congregation may even call one another to worship, but in reality God is the one who summons us from our scattered, individual lives and gathers us together to meet with him. Employing Scripture can help emphasize that God is the one gathering us together. A call to worship based on Psalm 84:1, for example, clearly establishes worship as a communal conversation with God: "How lovely is your dwelling place, LORD Almighty!" Several other psalms contain a call to worship that can be used effectively to begin a service, for example, Psalm 9:1-2; 66:1-4; 95:1-3, 6-7; 96–101; 103:1-6; 104:1; 105:1-4.

A meaningful prayer can also serve as an effective call to worship. *The Book of Common Worship* contains a rich collection of opening prayers, my favorite reads as follows:

> Almighty God,
> you pour out the spirit of grace and supplication
> on all who desire it.
> Deliver us from cold hearts and wandering thoughts,
> that with steady minds and burning zeal
> we may worship you in spirit and in truth;
> through Jesus Christ our Lord. Amen.

Directly addressing God from the start of the service reinforces one of the foundational principles of worship—that worship is a give-and-take conversation between God and his people.

While the *Word* portion of the four-tiered structure is taken up largely by the sermon, it also includes any Scripture readings, Bible-based prayers, or music that proclaims the Word of God. The purpose of the Word segment is to enable the people to hear from the Lord and, as a result, be edified, renewed, and ultimately transformed (2 Timothy 3:16-17; Romans 12:2). In chapter seven we will examine in greater detail the role of Scripture in corporate worship.

The *Table* segment functions as a response to the Word. Because gathered worship is dialogical, God's speaking to us through his Word merits a response. The combination of Word and Table echoes the pattern of communication— revelation followed by response—that is common to all divine-human encounters throughout Scripture. Churches that do not observe weekly Communion often substitute a song, prayer, or exhortation as an alternate response to the sermon. Chapter nine will discuss more fully the Lord's Supper as a spiritually formative corporate practice.

Directly addressing God from the start of the service reinforces one of the foundational principles of worship—that worship is a give-and-take conversation between God and his people.

The *sending* is usually the shortest segment of the service but is by no means insignificant, for it too has transforming potential. God, who called us together, now sends us out. The sending, therefore, like every other part of the service, is a response to God's initiative and God's actions. Whether spoken or sung, the sending is commonly divided into two brief statements: a *call to service* and a *benediction*. The sending essentially empowers worshipers to do God's will by blessing them with the assurance that God's presence and power remain with them as they leave church.

The call to service (also known as the charge) sends the people out with a sense of mission. It can be as simple as, "Go in peace to love and serve the Lord" or as involved as an extended exhortation from Scripture like Micah 6:8, Matthew 28:19-20, Acts 1:8, or Hebrews 13:20-21. In the same way that a call to worship drawn from Scripture conveys that God is the one gathering his people together, a Scripture-based call to service emphasizes that God is now sending us out to actively participate with him in fulfilling his mission on earth.

The benediction is a blessing spoken over the people before they depart and go their separate ways. The Aaronic blessing is most popular:

> The Lord bless you
>> and keep you;
> the Lord make his face shine on you
>> and be gracious to you;
> the Lord turn his face toward you
>> and give you peace. (Numbers 6:24-26)

Other examples are Matthew 28:19-20, Acts 1:8, 2 Corinthians 13:14, 2 Thessalonians 2:16-17, and Hebrews 13:20-21. A benediction drawn from Scripture is heard as God himself sending the people out with his blessing.

The way a service ends communicates a great deal about how we are to live and what we are to do throughout the week as God's people in the world. To close the service merely by dismissing everyone leaves the impression that worship is not only terminated for the time being but that it's also detached from the rest of life. The sending is more than a signal that church is over. Instead, it conveys that we're simply moving from one scene to another in a life of continual worship. Rather than the end, it is the beginning of our service in the world. An effective sending reminds us to live lives of worship throughout the week.

Because the flow of the four movements was originally orchestrated to reflect the formative journey of the Emmaus disciples, it holds great potential for spiritual transformation for all Jesus' disciples living this side of the resurrection. The order itself, of course, is not what changes lives and causes spiritual growth; the Holy Spirit is God's agent of transformation. The four guideposts—gathering, Word, Table, and sending—simply provide a useful road map for transforming worship by enabling every part of the service, not just the sermon, to contribute to a potentially formative experience.

REVIVALIST TEMPLATE FOR WORSHIP

For the first sixteen hundred years of church history, Christian worship services were strictly patterned on the four movements of the Emmaus encounter and were predominantly liturgical, which is the format that Roman Catholic and liturgical churches still adhere to. Those who worship in nonliturgical, Pentecostal, free, or contemporary styles, however, may not be able to detect a clear iteration of gathering, Word, Table, and sending in their church's order of service, at least in the classic sense. The reason for the discrepancy can be traced to the influence of the frontier revival services that swept across America and Europe during the nineteenth century, the influence of which is still being felt today.

In the eighteenth and nineteenth centuries the vast American frontier presented Christians with a unique challenge. In Europe the church operated more or less as if people were born into Christianity. Baptized as infants, rarely as adults, everyone grew up Christian. The American church, on the other hand, was dealing with a booming population that was for the most part unchurched and uneducated; people were also scattered over large areas of land. One way to meet the challenge of reaching the lost was to hold church meetings, some of which became big social events lasting several days. These large-scale meetings served as the backdrop for America's two great religious awakenings.

America's great awakenings and the revivalists. During the eighteenth century, changes were afoot in the American church's methodology. During the First Great Awakening (c. 1725–1750), preachers started to teach that human beings had a certain amount of responsibility in their salvation. With the help of the Holy Spirit, people needed to choose to follow Christ. The Second Great Awakening (c. 1795–1835) developed this idea of personal choice further as church leaders began to stress that it was urgent for people to do something to be saved—make a decision, go forward, say a prayer. With such heavy emphasis on human effort, the importance of God's redemptive actions, and all that God accomplished to deliver humanity from sin and death became minimized. That said, in the eighteenth century the idea that Christianity is not something we're born into—that we have to decide to follow Christ—was truly revitalizing the church.

Reflecting the evangelistic fervor of the day, Charles Finney, who became known as the father of modern revivalism, insisted that the church "should not sit back idly and wait for revival to mysteriously fall from the sky." Finney urged Christians to venture into the towns and surrounding countryside and evangelize aggressively. He instituted what he called "new measures" or new ways of doing ministry that included revival meetings, door-to-door witnessing, and sharing personal testimonies. One of Finney's most famous innovations was "the anxious bench." Those who were anxious about their salvation or who wanted to talk to someone about spiritual things were encouraged to sit in a special area (usually in front) during the meeting. Leaders were readily available to pray with those who were searching for God and answer their questions. The revivalists took the needs of unchurched people seriously.

Revivalism's threefold service order. Finney and company adopted a threefold, nonliturgical approach to planning revival meetings as the most effective way to reach unbelievers for Christ. Revival services began with what Finney referred to as "the preliminaries," which included songs, hymns, readings, and dramatic presentations—all designed to prepare the people to hear the sermon, which was the main attraction. The service concluded with a challenge or decision time, during which unbelievers were encouraged to decide for Christ, much like the modern altar call. Reflecting on the American proclivity for pragmatism, Finney defended his new approach by arguing that "nothing biblical or historical is normative except that which works at the present." His insistence that God did not establish "any particular form or manner of worship" in any church flies in the face of the biblical evidence and historical support for the fourfold outline for worship. In his later years Finney came to regret such youthful brashness, but throughout his life he remained the consummate pragmatist who believed that the end justifies the means, especially if the result meant winning more souls for Christ.

Finney's three-pronged structure—songs, sermon, closing—was soon adopted by various churches and by the late nineteenth century became the norm for evangelical and Pentecostal congregations (see fig. 2.2).

Figure 2.2. Revivalists' threefold order of service

Some of you may recognize this as the basic order of service at your church. Since the form and function of many Protestant church services are derived from America's frontier era, the influence of the revivalist movement on modern worship cannot be overstated.

Contemporary worship's binary order of service. Also rooted in nineteenth-century revivalism and especially popular among today's megachurches is the simple two-part service, which is song and sermon. In this streamlined version of the revivalist paradigm, the song portion is longer and much more substantial than Finney's preliminaries. The explosion of new praise music in the late twentieth century sparked worship renewal in churches throughout the world. Church music became more participatory and less presentational. Instead of watching soloists or a choir perform, the congregation is expected to sing along with a worship team. The first half of the service took on a life of its own. What came to be known as "the worship set" is an extended time of uninterrupted congregational singing featuring contemporary worship choruses. Today, Sunday services in churches without a traditional liturgy can be broken down into two main parts: worship set and sermon (see fig. 2.3).

Figure 2.3. Contemporary binary order of service

The simple two-part format outlined in figure 2.3 is popular these days for several reasons. Because modern worship choruses are accessible and singable, people can participate instead of spectating. These simple choruses enable churchgoers to express their personal thoughts and feelings to the Lord. As a result, many find the expanded time of praise singing to be deeply meaningful. I contend, however, that the "worship set" flowing into the sermon, as a structure for Sunday gatherings, is not as believer edifying as the classic fourfold template. The fact that the binary form lacks a distinct gathering that calls God's people to worship and a clear sending that releases them back into the wider world with a mission represents a missed opportunity for spiritual formation. Perhaps it's unfair to compare the two models. After all, the binary service evolved from frontier revivalism, which put a premium on evangelism, while the four-part structure was originally designed to edify believers. That doesn't mean that God can't use the simplest worship set and sermon for his good purposes. God is God. He has certainly proven that he is neither beholden to set forms and structures nor bound by human insufficiency. But as leaders our goal is to partner with God by offering services that are intentionally formative. To that end I'd like to suggest an alternative that preserves the spiritually formative aspects of the fourfold structure but takes into account the way many churches currently approach service planning.

FIVE-PART TEMPLATE FOR TODAY'S TRANSFORMING WORSHIP SERVICE

I propose a fivefold approach for transforming worship: call to worship, worship set, sermon, Table, sending. Each of these five segments flows seamlessly into the next and contributes effectively to a spiritually formative approach to worship (see fig. 2.4).

Figure 2.4. Five-part transforming worship order

The *call to worship* welcomes churchgoers into God's presence and establishes the gathering as a dynamic dialogue between God and his people. This opening to the service could take the form of a song, video, Scripture reading, prayer, or some combination thereof. The purpose of the *worship set* is to proclaim who God is and all that God has done, which puts heavy emphasis on the attributes of God and God's marvelous deeds. In addition to music, liturgy, prayer, and Scripture, this portion of the service can contain a wide variety of creative or spontaneous elements such as video, personal testimony, and dramatic presentation. I should clarify here that by adhering to the ubiquitous term *worship set*, I do not mean to suggest that it is the only time during the service when worship happens, for I strongly believe that every element of the service is indeed worship.

Continuing my overview of the fivefold template, the *sermon*, of course, offers biblical instruction and the *Table* reenacts God's saving act of redemption through Jesus Christ. In keeping with ancient tradition, the *sending* dispatches congregants to continue a vibrant life of worship outside the church during the week. I propose the fivefold structure as a viable way to combine the traditional order of service with a contemporary sensibility to achieve a compellingly formative worship experience for today's church.

WHAT DOES A FIVEFOLD ORDER OF SERVICE LOOK LIKE IN YOUR SETTING?

I'm convinced that the fivefold order is well-suited for both liturgical and nonliturgical settings. It's easily adoptable because it retains much, if not all, of what these churches are already doing while enhancing their services by offering more freedom, clarity, and intentionality to spiritual formation. In some cases it's simply a matter of different language (e.g., *sermon* instead of *Word*) to reflect current nomenclature. Churches are free, of course, to use whatever labels suit their settings.

For liturgical churches, for example, the fivefold paradigm preserves the traditional service order but allows for an extended time of singing within the liturgy. For nonliturgical churches, the fivefold format adds a dedicated call to worship at the beginning and a sending at the end of a typical contemporary service. Churches that don't observe weekly Communion could insert an appropriate response to the sermon, such as a song, prayer, or spiritual exercise.

Since the worship set is the distinctive feature of the fivefold service, it warrants more consideration. Featuring an extended time of singing every week has caused many churches to design worship sets with a specific purpose, goal, or destination in mind. I'd like to briefly analyze the three most popular types of worship sets today and note the strengths and weaknesses of each one. Pointing out their weaknesses does not disqualify any of them. I'm merely trying to alert leaders to deficiencies that they might want to ameliorate. I'm also not advocating one approach over the others. I'd encourage leaders to use all three of these methods—mix and match as you see fit. Instead of using the same strategy for your worship set every week, vary it. On any given Sunday, worship planners could employ any one of the following options. This list is not comprehensive but is a general overview. Worship sets today are usually some variation of one of these three basic typologies.

Topical worship set. One popular strategy involves planning the worship time around the same theme as the sermon. For example, the service could revolve around a timely topic, the big idea behind a Scripture passage, or an intriguing statement or question. The thought here is that the music and other elements prepare the congregation to hear the message and help drive home its main points. Focusing every part of the morning on the same theme enables the various elements to flow logically from one to the next resulting in a cohesive, well-integrated service.

One drawback to a service that focuses tightly on an idea is that it can come across as didactic, cognitive, or heady, leaving little or no opportunity for emotional engagement. Congregation members may not automatically make the connection between a certain song and the sermon because they haven't heard the sermon yet. If we're not careful, this strategy could produce a service that is about something other than one that is fundamentally an encounter with God. Also, as I've discovered over the years, not every topic lends itself well to a worship experience. For example, there might be very few songs written about a particular subject let alone good songs. On more than one occasion I've been proud of the fact that I found a song that fits a difficult topic, but the song fell completely flat in the service because it was not well-crafted; it was a boring song.

Worship-themed set. Another common plan calls for a praise time built around a worship-oriented theme, such as a specific attribute of God. Putting the spotlight completely on the Lord enables worshipers to experience God in a meaningful way. In this paradigm the worship set stands on its own; it may or may not have anything to do with the sermon. The assumption here is that if people are allowed to engage with the Lord meaningfully in worship they'll naturally be receptive to the sermon. Sometimes an attribute of God that is loosely associated with the sermon topic can be highlighted. A message based on the prodigal son, for example, could easily inspire a worship set emphasizing God's unrelenting love or grace.

While this approach gives significant priority to worship, one disadvantage to it stems from our tendency to focus on a small range of divine attributes. It's easy to find praise songs about God's goodness, love, mercy, or grace; those are common themes in Christian contemporary music. It is much more difficult to locate well-crafted songs about God's justice, transcendence, immutability, sovereignty, wisdom, omniscience, omnipotence, or omnipresence. The challenge then is not to allow the limits of Christian music to prevent us from experiencing the full spectrum of God's attributes.

Outer court to inner court worship set. Originating in the 1980s among Pentecostal and non-White churches, an outer-court-to-inner-court worship set reenacts what worshipers from ancient Israel experienced as they moved from the outer courts to the inner sanctum of the temple into the holy of holies. Song lyrics in this approach generally move from a horizontal to vertical point of view. In other words, the opening songs begin with "we" and "our" as the reference point but transition to "I" and "me" by the end of the worship set. Throughout the worship time, the congregation switches from talking to each other about God to addressing God personally.

To illustrate further, the old Vineyard model based on this concept begins with up-tempo songs of invitation that function as a call to worship, then moves to songs of exaltation highlighting God's attributes, continues with slower songs of adoration, and climaxes with mellow, quiet songs fostering intimacy with God. The goal here is for worshipers to enjoy a personal, intimate experience with the Lord. The Vineyard version of this approach often includes some kind of "ministry moment," during which the worship leader takes on more of a pastoral role and provides comments or guidance. The leader might also invite the congregation to reflect on a word or phrase from the song or come forward for prayer. A song might be elongated to draw out its deeper meaning. The ministry moment is designed to help worshipers connect with the Lord in a personal way.

Another adaptation of the outer-court-to-inner-court worship set is based on Psalm 100. The invitation in the psalm to enter God's gates with thanksgiving and his courts with praise (v. 4) is interpreted as a progression or journey from thanksgiving to praise to worship. The distinction here between praise and worship is intentional. Some churches define praise as acknowledging God's attributes and recounting God's actions. Worship, on the other hand, is viewed as expressing love and affection for God or Jesus.

In yet another variant of this design, also known as the temple-based worship set, some churches have modified the destination point. Instead of ending in a highly personal frame of mind, the worship journey ends with songs that are distinctly ascriptive. In other words the lyrics, instead of emphasizing "me," "my," or "I," focus solely on God. The idea here is that if we are truly standing in the holy of holies, our attention should be fixed on the Lord, not on ourselves.

The outer-court-to-inner-court music set, in all its different forms, is popular these days because it offers a meaningful experience that engages both the heart and the mind while fostering a personal encounter with the living God. There are some things to watch out for with this strategy though. The intense focus on the intimate and personal could cause worship to become "all about me" if we're not careful. Also if the worship set climaxes with a highly charged, passionate song that tugs at the heartstrings every Sunday, it could become formulaic, predictable, or worse, emotionally manipulative.

Since this approach is based on an Old Testament model, one important theological truth that could get lost is that Jesus is the one who makes it possible for us to stand in the holy of holies (Hebrews 10:19). A lack of clarity on this point, plus our heavy dependence on music, could leave worshipers with the wrong impression that sung praise, not the blood of Christ, is what ushers us into the presence of God.

I hope that the preceding summary opens your mind to new possibilities in planning worship sets. While the other parts of the service tend to be fixed and somewhat predictable, the worship set allows for a great deal of freedom and flexibility in planning. A well-crafted worship set is purposeful, creative, and brimming with variety.

3

HOW TO EDIFY BELIEVERS AND EVANGELIZE UNBELIEVERS

❧

I STARTED DRINKING COFFEE a few years ago. Until then I couldn't stand the taste of coffee. But one day I agreed to meet a young worship-leader friend at a gourmet coffee shop in downtown Omaha. As he was pointing out his favorite coffee choices on the menu, I interrupted and politely explained that I'd be ordering tea because I don't drink coffee. He looked at me with that incredulous expression I get when I tell young people that we used to write letters by hand, stick them in the mailbox, and wait five business days for a response. He couldn't believe that I was sitting in a gourmet coffee shop and not ordering coffee.

"Let me order you some coffee," he said with a gleam in his eye.

Minutes later our coffee arrived in fancy glassware. The slender beaker looked more like a high school science experiment than a cup o' joe. I took one sip and a whole new world opened up to me. My taste buds rose up and shouted, "Where have you been all my life? We've been drinking tea all these years instead of coffee! What were you thinking?"

Needless to say, I was shocked. "Is this what coffee is supposed to taste like?" I asked.

My young friend smiled. "It's Chemex," he proudly explained, which I later learned is a hoity-toity method of coffee brewing. My friend then proceeded to give me the entire spiel about how Americans drink burnt coffee and the only way to enjoy the full benefits of this miracle drink is to grind your beans and brew it yourself.

At that point I was hooked. I didn't care what it would take. I had tasted real coffee. No more settling for second best. I wanted the real thing. Ever since that fateful day in Omaha, I have been an impassioned coffee snob.

The New Testament doesn't describe in detail how the first Christians conducted worship services. At best, it offers glimpses here and there of what transpired when the church gathered. If we put those clues together, though, we get a sense—a taste—of what worship is supposed to be. A model emerges that we can emulate and follow, a model so compelling we no longer want to settle for the status quo; we want the real thing when it comes to worship.

This chapter presents a biblical model for transforming worship. To put the biblical blueprint into our modern context, we begin by examining the two most influential models in contemporary worship today. Over the last forty years, two approaches to service planning have dominated church worship—the *seeker-attractional* and *participatory-worship* models. Both paradigms separate believers from unbelievers and focus on one or the other. As we shall see, Scripture offers a third model that effectively addresses the spiritual needs of both. Let's begin by examining the strengths and weaknesses of both the seeker-attractional and participatory-worship philosophies of ministry.

SEEKER-ATTRACTIONAL MODEL

The seeker-attractional model is specially designed to appeal to unchurched people. Characterized as seeker-friendly or seeker-sensitive, this paradigm favors "event evangelism," wherein congregation members invite their unsaved friends to a well-polished, professional-quality church service or event, and the gospel or a seeker-friendly program is presented. I was part of the original youth group that began Willow Creek Community Church, which pioneered the seeker movement that became popular during the 1980s. I had the privilege of serving as the church's music director for twenty years and remain forever grateful for the years I spent there. Willow was not just seeker-sensitive; we were seeker-driven. We specifically targeted unbelievers—"unchurched Harry and Mary," as we fondly called them. We had countless conversations about the music unchurched Harry and Mary might listen to, the concerts they'd attend, and the TV shows they were likely to watch. We wanted to stay in touch with the culture so we could communicate effectively to our target audience. Weekend services were highly evangelistic. Many churches today subscribe to the attractional model; their methods may differ from Willow's, but their programming still aggressively targets unbelievers first and foremost on Sunday morning.

While seeker-attractional churches boast high numbers of new converts, their critics proclaim that this methodology dumbs down or even compromises spiritual truth for fear of offending non-Christians. And because seeker-sensitive ministries target unbelievers, the spiritual needs of Christians often remain unmet. Discipleship, for example, is accomplished through a separate meeting during the week featuring Bible study and worship or via small groups. At the height of the seeker movement, we saw thousands come to Christ at Willow. Meanwhile, attendance at "New Community" (the midweek believer service) and participation in small groups lagged far behind their weekend counterparts. A four-year research project chronicled in the book *Reveal: Where Are You?* surveyed thousands of Willow attendees and affirmed what those of us who worked there suspected all along—that Willow was a great place to find the Lord but not a great place to grow in the Lord. In all fairness to Willow, the spiritual needs of believers were not entirely ignored on weekends. Sermons often presented biblical truths relevant to both seekers and seasoned believers. It would be accurate to say, though, that Willow's weekend services put the needs of unbelievers at the forefront while the concerns of Christians came in a distant second.

In addition to the lack of discipleship, Timothy Keller lists several characteristics of the seeker-attractional approach that are opposed to the values of today's young pastors and the next generation of Christians:

1. Seeker services tend to target a narrow band of people (i.e., college-educated, white, baby-boomer suburbanites), but the next generation of unchurched people is multiethnic, diverse, and more urban-oriented.

2. The attractional model typically opts for upbeat, happy, light, contemporary music, but people today long for transcendence and a sense of awe from their religious experience.

3. Seeker churches dismiss history and tradition as irrelevant and champion anything and everything contemporary and current, but today's culture yearns for rootedness and prefers joining ancient and modern thought and practice.

4. The seeker paradigm highlights technical excellence, professionalism, and business management techniques while the younger generation values authenticity and community.

5. Sermons in the seeker mode typically present rational arguments, how-to philosophical advice, and step-by-step problem-solving techniques, but the next generation is attracted instead to narrative and that which is personal and authentic.

Despite their high number of converts, seeker-attractional services are not only ineffective in building up believers but also out of step with current culture and the next generation of unbelievers.

PARTICIPATORY WORSHIP MODEL

Another popular option for service planning today is the participatory worship model, which is, in some ways, a reaction against the perceived slickness and lack of spiritual depth found in the seeker movement. Participatory worship features passionately expressive praise music followed by a biblically based sermon. Participation is a high value in this paradigm; congregational singing trumps solos. The idea of a target audience makes no sense here, for it implies that people are supposed to spectate instead of participating. An extended time of worship singing is intended to draw believers into a personal encounter with Jesus. Sermons in this context offer practical and relevant biblical teaching to edify believers.

Worship-driven churches tend to shy away from evangelistic methods of previous generations, like event evangelism and seeker services. Instead, congregation members are challenged to build relationships with and minister to unchurched people at work and in the community. As they go about their daily activities rubbing shoulders with non-Christians, believers are encouraged to pray for and stay alert for opportunities to share their faith. Because evangelism is supposed to happen during the week, it doesn't factor heavily, if at all, into a participatory worship service.

The glaring weakness of this model is that it tends to make the needs of believers too much of a priority. To serve their people many churches offer different kinds of services, each with its unique style to accommodate the various musical preferences of the congregation. Though well-intentioned, catering to personal preferences fosters a consumeristic mindset in churchgoers. It conditions people to associate worship solely with music. Instead of something they offer God, worship becomes an experience to enjoy if—and only if—they like the music. At the same time, sermons that constantly address the felt needs of the congregation can convey a narrow and shallow view of discipleship.

Another drawback to this model is its failure to adequately address the needs of seekers on Sunday morning. One young pastor told me recently that he "loathes evangelism," so his church has adopted a missional approach to evangelism that separates it from worship. While I respect this view, I believe it's unrealistic to expect church members to carry the weight of evangelism during the week without any support from Sunday services. It's shortsighted to assume that worship can't play its unique role in reaching lost people. At the very least, gathered worship can effectively supplement a church's evangelistic efforts.

As we've seen, both models are seriously flawed; seeker-attractional services promote evangelism at the expense of edification, and participatory worship advocates edification at the expense of evangelism. My critique is not intended to be harsh or accusatory, and I'm speaking, of course, in general terms. Not all attractional churches lack effective discipleship, and not all worship-driven churches neglect the lost. My purpose here is to draw attention to an underlying issue facing service planners: Is it possible to edify and evangelize on Sunday morning? If so, what does that look like? Is it a matter of equal time given to each? Does one take precedence over the other? If so, what is the proper balance? To illustrate what it looks like to address the needs of both the churched and the unchurched during worship, I suggest we drop in for a visit to the ancient city of Corinth.

WELCOME TO CORINTH

Scripture offers a fascinating glimpse through the window of a prominent first-century church on a Sunday morning. Toward the end of a four-chapter discourse on establishing order in worship, Paul writes, "If an unbeliever or an inquirer comes in while everyone is prophesying, they are convicted of sin and are brought under judgment by all, as the secrets of their hearts are laid bare. So they will fall down and worship God, exclaiming, 'God is really among you!'" (1 Corinthians 14:24-25).

Whether Paul is reporting what he actually witnessed or writing hypo-thetically, he paints a vivid picture of a non-Christian experiencing a meaningful, life-altering encounter with God at a church service. Reading this passage in the context of Paul's entire letter reveals that the Corinthian church was able to edify believers and evangelize un-believers on Sunday morning. Let's consider how they accomplished both at the same time.

Edify believers. Throughout 1 Corinthians 14, Paul repeatedly states that the purpose of a Christian worship gathering is the edification of the believer (vv. 3-5, 12, 17, 26). Spiritual gifts were to be used for building up others. Paul conceived of public worship as a highly partici-patory, spontaneous event where everyone came with a song, a teaching, a story, a word from God to minister to fellow believers (v. 26). The apostle instructed the Christians in Rome to "make every effort" to do that which leads to "mutual edification" whenever they gathered (Romans 14:19).

When Paul was with the Corinthians he modeled a preaching style that stressed Christ crucified (1 Corinthians 1:23). Sunday sermons at the First Church of Corinth were far from trite or shallow; these were not watered down, self-help messages. They centered on Christ and his saving work in our lives and in the world. Paul did not edify worshipers by addressing their heart-felt needs but by directing their attention to Christ. Church services at Corinth contained sub-stantive, spiritually formative content specifically designed to build up believers.

Evangelize unbelievers. Paul seems to assume that non-Christians would be present at a worship service, which is a rather extraordinary assumption given that early church gatherings were not designed to at-tract unbelievers; they were not seeker-sensitive at all. Evangelism in Paul's day was a grassroots effort that happened quite naturally as be-lievers developed relationships with unbelievers. Eventually, Christians would invite their non-Christian family members, friends, neighbors, and coworkers to church.

The fact that nonbelievers could be in attendance is one of the reasons Paul warned the Corinthians to restore order to their services. Their worship gatherings had become chaotic. People were speaking in tongues, for example, with no interpretation. Paul was worried that the congregation wouldn't understand what they were hearing, that instead of receiving a meaningful word from God, people would hear nothing but unintelligible gibberish (1 Corinthians 14:9). It was customary for worshipers to chime in together and shout "Amen!" in agreement after each prophetic word; if people couldn't understand what was being said, they couldn't reply with a hearty amen (1 Corinthians 14:16). In other words, they wouldn't be able to participate in the service. Paul was especially concerned about outsiders who came to church out of curiosity or at the invitation of a friend or relative (1 Corinthians 14:24). Visitors would be lost and confused. Paul wanted everyone who walked through the church doors to feel welcome and included. He called on the leaders at Corinth to ensure that every part of the worship experience was intelligible and comprehendible.

BIBLICAL MODEL FOR TRANSFORMING WORSHIP

Paul's instructions to the Corinthians shed light on the edification versus evangelism controversy; it's not an either-or proposition but a both-and opportunity. More importantly, Paul establishes clear priorities in the matter: when it comes to church services, the first priority is believers; the second priority is unbelievers. Seekers are a concern, but not the top concern. Encouraging the congregation to reach out to unbelievers during the week takes the pressure off Sunday services to carry the evangelistic freight, as it does with the attractional model. Though worship services are not meant to be seeker-driven, they can still support and supplement outreach.

Before I get into how Sunday services can do that, allow me to address a concern that some might have regarding the Corinthian church. We all know the Corinthians had their problems. There was, as I said, disorder and chaos whenever they gathered. They were also divided (1 Corinthians 1:10-13), sexual immorality was rampant (1 Corinthians 5:1-5), they were filing lawsuits against each other (1 Corinthians 6:1-6), they were confused on spiritual issues (1 Corinthians 8), and they were abusing the Lord's Supper (1 Corinthians 11:17-33). In other words the Corinthian church was not perfect. Far from it. But then again, what church is? Yet Paul gives them a vision for worship that effectively evangelizes unbelievers in the context of a believers' service. This transformative view of worship is just as relevant to us today as it was to the first generation of Christians, for it combines the best of both the attractional and participatory models. Let's discuss what it looks like to evangelize unbelievers in the context of our own believers' service.

The transformative view of worship combines the best of both the attractional and participatory models.

EVANGELIZING UNBELIEVERS IN A BELIEVERS' SERVICE

Though unbelievers are not the priority in a transforming worship service, reaching them requires an effective strategy. Non-Christians do not normally come to church unless they're invited by someone who already attends. By the same token believers do not normally invite guests unless they're confident the first-timers will find the service to be a positive and meaningful experience. It's a vicious cycle, observes Tim Keller; leaders don't see unbelievers among the congregation so there's no incentive to accommodate them, and at the same time, church members don't think to invite anyone because they fear their friends and relatives won't be impressed. The best way to get Christians to bring their non-Christian friends and relatives is to plan and lead worship as if there were a significant number of skeptical, uninitiated onlookers. When we continually worship as if there are seekers in the room, eventually they will be there in reality. Churches need to devise strategies for reaching seekers on Sunday morning not only so they'll come, but, more importantly, so believers will feel comfortable inviting them. Here are four suggestions regarding planning and leading worship as if seekers are present.

Spiritual formation is intrinsic to what it means to be saved; it is not an optional add-on.

Help seekers feel welcome. First, demonstrate hospitality to unbelievers in your midst. Guests and visitors should feel welcome. They should be warmly greeted when they arrive. Signage or clear directions should be given regarding parking, and someone should always be readily available to answer any questions. The building and all facilities should be neat and clean. The service itself, especially the music, should be done with as much excellence as possible. Doing everything you can reasonably do to make your church attractive to outsiders assures believers that your church is a safe place they can bring their unsaved friends and family members to.

When I'm on assignment as a worship consultant and I visit a church for the first time, I try to look at the experience through the eyes of an outsider. Was it easy or difficult to park, find the entrance, and know where to go? Could families figure out where to drop off their kids? Was I accosted at the door or greeted cordially? Was someone readily available to answer questions? Was I able to find a seat? Was the service easy to follow, or was I lost most of the time? Were there any inside jokes or jargon from the front that went unexplained and made me feel left out? Consider what it's like for non-Christians to come to your church on a typical Sunday morning.

I need to include one caveat about making unbelievers feel welcome and comfortable. They will never be completely comfortable because the cross—preaching Christ crucified as Paul put it—is not seeker-sensitive. The unbelieving Corinthian that Paul cited certainly wasn't made to feel comfortable. Convicted of sin, he came face-to-face with his own depravity, which undoubtedly made him feel exposed and ashamed. But that's exactly the kind of God-graced repentance that leads to salvation. We need to be sensitive to the needs of unsaved people without compromising the gospel message.

Worship like you mean it. Scripture encourages God's people to sing praises before the nations of the world (2 Samuel 22:50; Psalm 18:49). God wants unbelievers to overhear us worshiping him. Passionate and dynamic worship is one of the most effective forms of Christian witness. I've heard pastors tell their people to "tone it down" during worship so as not to scare off seekers. If the Corinthian visitor's experience proves anything, it's that worship can be evangelistic. An assembly of fired-up, expressive Christians singing God's praises from the top of their lungs communicates that God is alive, present, and active in our world. Encourage your worship team and your congregation to worship like they mean it as an effective witness for Christ.

By the same token I don't recommend altering, avoiding, or dumbing down biblical teaching for fear of offending seekers. Unsaved people want to hear the truth about God; that's why they come to church in the first place. We should not allow concern for turning off unbelievers to prevent Christians from doing what Christians typically do when we get together. We need to remain authentic in worship and be ourselves every Sunday, which means we sing, we pray, we lift high the name of Jesus, we open the Word of God, we receive Communion. And we do all of those things unapologetically and passionately. We should be sensitive to the needs of non-Christians, but not compromise biblical truth or alter who we are in the process.

Help seekers understand. We need to make sure that all we say and do during worship is comprehendible to outsiders. Paul was adamant that seekers at Corinth understand what was happening throughout the service so they could participate. Some parts of the service might need to be explained to non-Christians. For example, explain why we sing, pray, receive an offering, or baptize. Before a prayer, a pastor or worship leader could address seekers directly and say something like, "If you're new to prayer, we're just talking to God right now, so feel free to join us if you'd like." Never coerce, manipulate, or demand the congregation to do something. Always treat people with respect, and be polite. Invite worshipers to participate but allow them not to join in if they're not ready to do so.

Present conversion from a biblical perspective. There is an alarming number of people who claim they've been Christians for years but lack spiritual maturity and live nominal Christian lives. Part of the problem is that we have done a poor job of articulating what becoming a Christian entails. Too often we urge unbelievers to accept Christ without mentioning how their lives can be transformed over time. Many come to Christ assuming that discipleship is optional. If all that people have to do is ask Jesus into their hearts and they're saved, then why should they bother with spiritual formation? Why should anyone take discipleship seriously if they're already going to heaven? Our lack of clarity results in an incomplete view of Christian conversion. As a result, people may come to Christ but very few experience significant transformation.

Scripture indicates that salvation is more than what we experience at the initial point of conversion. We are instructed to grow in our salvation (1 Peter 2:2) through a lifelong process of rebirth and renewal by the Holy Spirit (Titus 3:5). The regenerative nature of biblical salvation—being given new life in Christ (Romans 6:4)—coincides with Jesus' invitation to be born again (John 3:3-5). This process of regeneration does not happen overnight; it takes time. Martin Luther taught that our life on earth "is not righteousness but growth in righteousness; not health, but healing; not being but becoming; not rest, but exercise; we are not yet what we shall be, but we are growing toward it; the process is not yet finished, but it is going on." The Christian experience is a lifelong process of being conformed to the image of Christ (Romans 8:29).

Conversion is so much more than merely saying the prayer or going forward during an altar call. It's a lifelong journey into wholeness in Christ; it's about growing in loving communion with God. Ruth Barton agrees that "salvation is not merely about making it to heaven when we die; it is about the possibility of kingdom living here and now." A sound theology of conversion envisions fallen human beings restored into the right relationship with God, and each one of us becoming a new person in Christ (2 Corinthians 5:17-18).

It is of vital importance that those of us who plan and lead worship offer our people a full-orbed conversion experience. We must convey that spiritual formation is intrinsic to what it means to be saved; it is not an optional add-on. It's okay for people to come to Jesus "just as I am" as long as they don't leave church thinking that it's okay to stay that way. Our songs, prayers, liturgies, and sermons should communicate that conversion is not the end but the beginning of an ongoing spiritual adventure that conforms believers to the likeness of Jesus Christ.

The Christian experience is a lifelong process of being conformed to the image of Christ.

4

RECLAIMING SUNDAY MORNING
AS THE CHURCH'S PRIMARY,
FORMATIVE EVENT

❧

S O FAR WE HAVE DISCOVERED that the concept of transforming
worship is rooted in Scripture. We've traced its origins to the book
of Exodus, specifically Mount Sinai, where we learned that transforming
worship is a God-initiated meeting between himself and his people that
is dialogical. During this highly participatory gathering, believers are to
do three things: (1) proclaim who God is and what he has done, (2) call
each other to remain faithful in our commitment to follow Christ, and
(3) reenact God's saving work of redemption. Chapter two added two
more principles: biblical worship is Christocentric and trinitarian. We
also derived a five-part template for transforming worship from the
Emmaus story in Luke 24, specially adapted for the modern church. In
chapter three, we visited the First Church of Corinth and learned that
transforming worship edifies believers first and foremost but also evangelizes unbelievers, and we discussed how to navigate the tension between these goals. Now we look at the historical foundations of
transforming worship. What happened after the New Testament? What
did church services look like? Did they continue to be spiritually

formative? To answer those questions we turn to the worship practices of the early church. By early church I'm referring to the first four centuries of church history, which, despite persecution, was a time of rapid growth for the upstart Christian community.

THE CHURCH'S PRIMARY, FORMATIVE EVENT

In his informative book *The Patient Ferment of the Early Church*, Alan Kreider traces the rise of Christianity from its heretical, cult status to empire-wide acceptance. One of the main reasons for this improbable rise in popularity was the impression that those first Christians made on the pagan world around them. The manner in which those embattled Christians lived out their beliefs—their character and conduct, especially under duress—resulted in a large number of their pagan neighbors converting to Christianity. Kreider proposes that the values and lifestyles of the earliest Christians were formed in part by the rigorous instruction they received in preparation for baptism but more regularly by what they learned and experienced at church every Sunday.

Historical documents confirm that the early church operated under the assumption that worship services were the ideal context to carry out its God-given mandate to make disciples of all the nations. The *Didache*, a first-century discipleship manual, exhorts believers to gather together frequently, "seeking the things pertaining to your souls." The earliest Christians came to church expecting to be fed spiritually.

During the first four centuries of the church, its leaders were at the forefront of formulating Christian doctrine, mostly in response to the heresies that threatened to undermine the emerging Jesus movement. Even a cursory glance at the writings and sermons from the patristic era reveals robust teaching on the Christian life. At the same time, the church's first theologians also functioned as local pastors tasked with the challenge of helping converted pagans grow in their newfound faith. These leaders took people born and raised in a pagan culture and sought to educate and train them so they could navigate the challenges of living the Christian lifestyle in a world that was antagonistic to the faith.

Sermons at this time were brief, practical, and to the point. The church's earliest preachers had a knack for making biblical truths and theological principles accessible to common people and applicable to their lives. The teaching offered at Sunday services was based on Scripture. Tertullian, one of the great early apologists of the faith, speaks of church members reading "the books of God" together to have their eyes opened to the truth and being strengthened in their faith as they inculcate or internalize God's Word.

Ancient church leaders labored under the assumption that Christian character is learned behavior, that acting like Christ does not come naturally to sin-prone human beings. "Christians are made, not born," insisted Tertullian. Around AD 155, Justin Martyr wrote a report for the emperor in which he describes a typical worship gathering at his church in Rome. After the Scripture reading, the church father notes that the presiding leader would deliver a speech in which he urged and invited believers to imitate the virtues revealed in the Scriptures. For our Christian ancestors, gathered worship was a consistent source of support and encouragement for learning and appropriating Christian virtues.

The early Christians may not have called it spiritual formation, but they were intentional about discipleship. More importantly, they purposely positioned Sunday morning as the church's primary, formative event. At that time, when a Christian wanted to grow in the Lord or stay on track spiritually, they faithfully attended weekly church services.

Formative Aspects of the Church Year

In addition to sermons, early church services imparted theological training through their prayers, Scripture readings, and creeds—elements the church eventually incorporated into a standard liturgy. Susan White contends that Christianity's liturgical tradition is based on the belief that the church's public worship constitutes the primary source of spiritual nourishment for Christian life. By the end of the fourth century the church had developed a three-year cycle of Scripture readings, which became known as the lectionary. Every Sunday four related passages were read—each one from a different section of the Bible such as the Old Testament, Psalms (spoken or sung), Gospels, and Epistles. Responsive readings, prayers, music selections, and even the sermon followed themes generated by the assigned Scriptures.

The lectionary was part of a seasonal cycle known as the "church year" or the "Christian year," which was developed explicitly with spiritual formation in mind. The church year captures the story of Jesus under three general headings: manifestation, resurrection, and indwelling Spirit. The church year presents the gospel, the story of Jesus, as the essence of Christian spirituality: Christ the Son manifests God the Father, Jesus rose from the dead and sent the Holy Spirit to indwell his followers. While most Catholic and mainline Protestant denominations still use the lectionary and follow the church year, many nondenominational churches are now adopting these proven tools as the framework for a spiritually formative approach to worship.

Church year spirituality. Because each season of the church year has a specific theme and emphasis, a distinctive spirituality developed for each of them. The Christian calendar divides into eight seasons: Advent, Christmas, Epiphany, Lent, the Great Triduum, Easter, and post-Pentecost. Each season has its own unique spiritual flavor.

Advent. In the Christian tradition, the new year begins not on January 1 but on the first Sunday of Advent, which occurs late November or early December. Advent, from the Latin *adventus*, means "coming" or "approaching" and alludes not only to God coming into the world through Jesus but also to the risen Christ's second coming in triumphant glory. Lasting about four weeks, Advent is a time of waiting for the coming of

Christ. For that reason churches following the church calendar do not sing Christmas carols during Advent for the simple reason that Christ has not come yet. Waiting to sing Christmas carols until Jesus is born is a countercultural statement in itself, but it also helps believers in our efforts to avoid the commercialism that typically surrounds Christmas. During Advent, Christians get in touch with their desire for God and our longing for redemption, which, for example, could prompt believers to identify any areas of bondage in their lives that they yearn to be set free from. Bernard of Clairvaux, a twelfth-century monk, spoke of three comings of Christ related to Advent: in the flesh at Bethlehem, daily in our hearts, and in the fullness of his resurrected glory at the end of the age. "In the first," writes Bernard, "Christ was our redemption; in the last, he will appear as our life; in the middle coming, he is our rest and consolation."

Christmas. The church began observing Christmas around the fourth century. But instead of honoring the Messiah's coming only one day out of the year, Christians have traditionally celebrated Christmas for twelve straight days. Importantly, Christ's coming in the flesh is not commemorated as some past event but as a present reality; for that reason the incarnation was established as a theme crucial for Christmas. The original purpose of Christmas was not to fixate on the baby Jesus but instead to contemplate the implications of Christ's incarnation. The fact that God accomplishes for humanity what we are unable to do for ourselves is a bedrock principle of our faith. Throughout the Christmas season believers are challenged to live with an incarnational mindset—to continually allow Jesus to dwell in us. The incarnation also proclaims that God unites himself to us so we can be united with God. Christmas essentially invites believers into transforming union with Christ.

Epiphany. After Christmas comes Epiphany, which means "appearance" or "manifestation." Churches in the East designated Epiphany as a celebration of Christ's baptism. In the West, however, Epiphany highlights the manifestation of Christ as realized in three major events:

the visit of the Magi, Christ's baptism, and the marriage feast at Cana. Epiphany invites us to consider how Christ is manifested in us and through us. In the same way that Jesus manifested himself to us, we are to manifest him to the world by the way we live.

Lent. Lent begins on Ash Wednesday and is a time of repentance and renewal. Three spiritual practices characterize the forty-day Lenten season: self-examination leading to repentance, Scripture meditation, and acts of self-denial such as fasting, prayer, and almsgiving. Fasting not only entails giving something up but also taking something on. A Lenten spirituality invites us to give up something that has too much control over us and replace it with a positive alternative such as a godly virtue. Lent therefore lends meaning and depth to Christian conversion by helping us to remain faithful in our commitment to follow Christ.

The Great Triduum. Next in the church year is the Great Triduum, also known as the Three Great Days, which include Maundy Thursday, Good Friday, and the Easter Vigil. The title for Maundy Thursday derives from the Latin *mandatum*, which means "command" or "mandate," stemming from the new commandment Jesus gave the disciples during the Last Supper—to love one another as he loved them (John 13:34-35). A foot-washing ceremony and a solemn observance of the Lord's Supper typify a worship service on the Thursday of Passion Week. The cross is emblematic of Good Friday, for it captures all the spiritual themes of Jesus' crucifixion: sacrifice, self-giving love, obedience, redemption, and atonement. In Christian tradition the Easter Vigil summons believers to stay awake and keep watch for Jesus' resurrection. Vigil services usually begin in the dark hours of Saturday night, continue until sunrise on Easter morning, and include extended liturgical readings, baptisms, and the Lord's Supper. Worship services during the Three Great Days are specially designed to enable believers to participate in these redemptive events through a unified sequence of dramatic reenactments, embodied actions, Scripture, and prayer.

Fifty days of Easter. In many nondenominational churches, Easter is a mammoth celebration—Christianity's great Super Bowl—but it lasts only one day. Churches adhering to the Christian Year, however, celebrate Christ's resurrection for a total of fifty days. The extended length is due to the fact that, after being raised from the dead, Jesus appeared to his disciples for forty days, after which he ascended into heaven (Acts 1:3). Ten days later, according to Acts 2, the Holy Spirit descended at Pentecost, which marks the end of the church's Easter season. God's victory over the powers of evil, specifically sin and death, is the main theme of Easter. Throughout the fifty days of Easter, Christians are invited to walk in the newness of life in the Holy Spirit.

Ordinary Time. The period after Easter is called Ordinary Time or simply the season after Pentecost and focuses heavily on the practical aspects of living the Christian life. Lectionary readings during this post-Pentecost period cycle somewhat continuously through several books of the Bible, so they might not always relate to each other. For this season some churches take a break from following the lectionary and concentrate instead on a specific biblical book of their choosing.

The season after Pentecost stretches through the summer and into the fall, ending on the first Sunday in Advent, when the cycle begins anew. Though it follows the same sequence of seasons every year, the church's calendar occurs in three iterations, cycles A, B, and C, each with its own set of Scriptures. Churches using the lectionary and following the Church Year go through the entire Bible then every three years.

The church calendar has proven to be a significant catalyst for spiritual growth.

Historical example of transforming worship. Robert Webber affirms that the original purpose of the church year was to guide Christians in their spiritual journeys. By inviting believers to relive the life of Christ, walk in Jesus' footsteps, experience what he experienced, and identify with his earthly life, the church calendar has proven to be a significant catalyst for spiritual growth. The church, then, has had a discipleship curriculum built into Sunday gatherings since its early stages. For two millennia the lectionary and the Christian Year have provided a framework for public worship that automatically generates a formative approach to corporate prayer, Scripture reading, confession, the Lord's Supper, and baptism. The early church, then, provides us with the finest historical example of a transforming worship service.

The Unique Role of Gathered Worship in Spiritual Formation

The ancient church knew what many today are discovering afresh—that gathered worship plays a vital role in spiritual formation. Maxwell Johnson contends that "Christians act morally or ethically because of what they believe, and what they believe is continually shaped by worship, by how they are formed by the words and acts of worship." Regardless of our church's tradition or style of music, its worship services help shape the hearts and minds of its people. Mike Cosper insists that our worship is "always teaching, shaping, and painting a picture of what the Christian life looks like." Let's explore briefly the role that worship plays in God's efforts to conform us to the image of Christ.

Gathered worship models essential spiritual practices. Since the beginning of our faith, Christians have practiced certain disciplines to enable themselves to be more present to God and therefore more open to God working in their lives. Robert Mulholland describes these spiritual disciplines as acts of faithful and loving obedience consistently offered to God "for whatever work God purposes to do in and through" us. Spiritual practices and rhythms help us to cooperate more fully with God's ongoing work of transformation in our lives (Philippians 2:12-13). They help us get out of God's way so he can bring us to full maturity in Christ. The disciplines themselves are never the end goal; they are a means to an end. They create space for God in our lives and open the door for deeper, life-altering intimacy with God.

Gathered worship offers us an opportunity to practice classic Christian disciplines such as prayer, Bible reading, worship, and confession alongside fellow believers. Church services, therefore, are habit-forming in that they help us form and maintain essential practices and rhythms that contribute to a vibrant walk with the Lord.

Gathered worship directs our desires toward God. One of the unique values of corporate spiritual practices—those experienced regularly on Sunday mornings—is that they shape and direct our desire for God in ways that private disciplines fail to replicate. In his book *Desiring the Kingdom*, James K. A. Smith argues that human beings are defined by what they ultimately love or desire above all else. This love or desire is aimed at an objective that represents our vision of the good life, of what it means to flourish as human beings. Humans are motivated, for better or for worse, by our inner longings. We may seek the fulfillment of our desires in things that eventually prove futile or not as life-giving as we thought they would be. And that's our choice. But whether consciously or subconsciously, our desires shape our thoughts, our actions, and give overall direction and meaning to our lives.

Spiritual practices and rhythms help us to cooperate more fully with God's ongoing work of transformation in our lives.

Smith explains further that our desires get aimed in specific directions by habitual behavior—habits, patterns, or practices that inevitably shape us. Our most influential routines—those that mark us most indelibly—are embodied actions, which are routines or practices experienced not cognitively but physically. Humans are not merely cerebral beings who just happen to have bodies. We are complex, embodied people whose primary orientation to the world is not cerebral but visceral. Habitual physical actions affect us on a gut level; they incorporate a type of training that is holistic and shape us often without our realizing it. In other words, that which affects our whole being, not just our minds, leaves the deepest impression. Over time, habits and rituals, combined with pertinent images and stories, reshape the way we relate to the world by molding and redirecting our desires.

Worship is one of those embodied habits that trains us to live in accordance with our desire for God; it keeps our desire for God on track, especially in the face of trial and temptation. Gathered worship fortifies our desire for the Lord because there is a unique physicality to it. Sung worship, for example, is physically demanding; it requires standing, deep breathing, and singing, sometimes even hand clapping. But in the process, music engages our emotions, evokes memories, and gets us in touch with how we truly feel. And singing is just one physical action experienced throughout a typical church service. We may also fold hands or kneel to pray; during the Lord's Supper we ingest the bread and the wine. At its best, gathered worship is a holistic, visceral event that helps keep our desires aimed Godward by connecting our minds to our bodies, our thoughts to our emotions.

Worship, therefore, enables us to experience our longing for God on a gut level—to the core of our being. Even when we allege that we didn't get anything out of church, just being there keeps our hearts and minds aimed in the direction of what we truly desire: a right relationship with God. When we include church attendance as part of our weekly routine, we're saying something significant about the kind of people we want to be and are trying to become. Private spiritual disciplines are of immense value for the spiritual life, but they do not shape our lives as holistically as corporate spirituality does. Regular participation in gathered worship is uniquely formative because it invites us to embrace—with all our heart, soul, and mind—our deepest desire for intimacy with God (Matthew 22:37).

It is time for third-millennium Christians to rediscover what the ancient church knew all along—that Sunday morning is the ideal setting for churchwide spiritual transformation and that gathered worship plays a vital role in the process of discipleship. The Sunday morning gathering is simply the most logical time for the church to carry out Jesus' mandate to form disciples. Weekend church services are the most highly attended meetings in the life of the church; because services are weekly, they are an established part of everyone's schedules. Relying solely on the small group ministry to form people spiritually will allow a church to influence only those who participate, which, in most cases, is a small percentage of the congregation. More church members are present on Sunday morning than any other day of the week, which makes it our best opportunity for spiritual growth. Since spiritual formation is the central work of the church, we need to reclaim Sunday morning as the church's primary, formative event.

> *Private spiritual disciplines are of immense value for the spiritual life, but they do not shape our lives as holistically as corporate spirituality does.*

SUNDAY MORNING AS YOUR CHURCH'S PRIMARY, FORMATIVE EVENT

The question facing those of us who plan and lead worship is, What does it look like to treat Sunday morning like it's your church's primary, formative event? For starters, it necessitates that the contents of our services be spiritually substantive—that the prayers we say, the songs we sing, the instruction we offer all reflect biblical theology and sound Christian doctrine. We will continue to probe in detail what that entails throughout the rest of this book.

I also suggest that twenty-first-century church leaders consider incorporating the lectionary and the Christian Year (or parts of them) into their services if they do not already do so. Experiencing Lent together as a church would be a great way to introduce your congregation to the Christian Year. Emphasize the spiritual dimension of each season and introduce a spiritual practice for each one. These time-tested tools can be valuable assets in our quest for a formative approach to weekend worship.

Earlier I mentioned that the early Christians were shaped and transformed by what they learned and experienced at church every Sunday, and they went on to turn their world upside down. Imagine what could happen if we in the twenty-first century followed historic church practice and once again decided to make Sunday morning the church's primary, formative event.

5

Recovering a Sense of the Sacred in Modern Worship

✥

S INCE OLD TESTAMENT TIMES, God's people have always depended on symbols, rituals, and sacred actions to keep their desires aimed Godward. Unfortunately, we Protestants tend to downplay the value of such things. Perhaps our reticence is rooted in the Reformation's objection to Roman Catholicism's veneration of relics. We don't want to be accused of worshiping things or inanimate objects. Insisting that the Bible is all one needs for spiritual living (*sola scriptura*), many Protestants view symbols and rituals as a crutch or a sign of spiritual weakness. Such narrow-mindedness is ironic given the fact that John Calvin, for example, regarded symbolism and ritual as God's way of accommodating our human weakness. The Reformer had no problem admitting that our faith is "slight and feeble," needing to be "propped on all sides and sustained by every means" God makes available. God understands how difficult it is for humans to put their faith in a God they can't see or touch, so he uses symbols—earthly things we can see and touch—to bring us to himself.

Symbols and Rituals in the Bible

Despite our resistance the Bible is loaded with symbolism and ritual. God instructed Old Testament patriarchs and leaders to build altars to commemorate specific blessings from the Lord (Noah: Genesis 8:20; Abraham: Genesis 12:7; Isaac: Genesis 26:25; Moses: Exodus 17:15). On the eve of their deliverance from slavery, God instructed the Israelites to prepare a Passover meal rich with symbols and actions (Exodus 12). Jewish fathers were required to explain to their children the meaning of each symbol and sacred act (Exodus 12:26-27; 13:8, 14). For example, bitter herbs were consumed as a reminder of the bitter harshness of slavery (Exodus 12:8). At Sinai, God instituted Israel's system for ritual sacrifice, which also integrated symbols and gestures. During the burnt offering, for example, worshipers were instructed to put a hand on the head of the animal to identify with it as their substitute sacrifice (Leviticus 1:4). God even designed Israel's mobile sanctuary, the tabernacle, with symbolic images, statues, furniture, and vestments for the priests (Exodus 25–28). In each of these cases the ritual and the symbol behind it were God's idea; when the Israelites went through these sacred routines, they were carrying out God's orders. The ancient Hebrews believed God is everywhere, but they were also convinced that whenever they gathered, they could experience the divine presence uniquely through the sacred symbols and rituals God instituted for them to observe.

Because of its Jewish heritage the early church naturally believed that God could be encountered through certain God-ordained material objects. The first Christians quickly adopted the cross as a symbol of Christ's death and resurrection. They also interpreted Jesus' baptism and the Last Supper as rituals he intentionally instituted for them to continue observing; water, bread, wine, and cup became meaningful symbols associated with baptism and the Lord's Supper. God established these rituals with all their symbolic actions as a viable way for God's people to experience his presence.

In chapter one we noted that one of the foundational functions of biblical worship is to reenact God's saving acts of deliverance. At Passover, Israel relived the miracle of God rescuing them from slavery; during the Lord's Supper, Christians remember Christ's death and resurrection in redeeming humanity from sin and death. For both Passover and Communion, God specified the physical elements to use, outlined a basic script to follow, and explained the meaning behind it all. Religious rituals and their symbols constitute a biblically sanctioned means of reenacting God's saving acts of deliverance during worship.

PROMINENCE OF SYMBOLISM AND RITUAL IN CULTURE

While Protestants deny the validity of symbols and rituals, modern culture recognizes both as a natural and meaningful part of life. Media and advertising constantly exploit the power of images and stories to sell a product or push an agenda. Even the world of sports is replete with symbols and routine actions. Trophies such as the Vince Lombardi Trophy, the Commissioner's Trophy, the Stanley Cup, and the World Cup symbolize championships. Baseball players go through their own set rituals every time they step into the batter's box. Sadly, our surrounding culture understands the power of symbols and stories more than we Protestants do.

Religious rituals and their symbols constitute a biblically sanctioned means of reenacting God's saving acts of deliverance during worship.

Symbols become meaningful because of what they represent. Nations revere their flags because they represent the shared history of their people. Every one of us attaches importance to certain objects or images because they remind us who we are and how we want to act. I wear a wedding ring because I'm a married man. I love my wife, value our relationship, and want to remain loyal to her for the rest of my life. The band I wear around my finger influences my behavior; it serves as a constant reminder to act like a married man. Flirting or fantasizing about other women is unacceptable behavior for me because I have a wife. The symbol is important to me because of what it signifies—my love for and commitment to my bride. So it's not about the ring, it's about all that the ring stands for.

In addition to symbols, rituals are also a part of everyday life. My wedding ring was placed on my finger during a special ceremony—a ritual—that took place on November 3, 1979. My wife and I have even established a little routine around that date. Early November every year we go out for dinner to celebrate our wedding anniversary. Whether we realize it or not, all of us have rituals we observe religiously—routines and habits that are regular parts of our daily lives or that are unique to special seasons of the year. At Christmas, for example, many families develop memorable rituals around obtaining a Christmas tree, decorating it, or opening presents, all of which lend greater meaning to the holiday.

Much is being written these days about the importance of rituals from an anthropological standpoint. Janine Morgan finds that rituals help shape people's beliefs, give us a sense of belonging, and ultimately determine behavior. During times of tragedy or turmoil, shared narratives and rituals become especially important as a means of anchoring families, communities, and nations in significant living truths. Timothy Son also appreciates the anchoring influence of ritual in determining beliefs, belonging, and behavior and insists that "ritual can no longer be considered as a senseless activity, but rather one of many ways in which human beings construe and construct meanings about their world." Symbols and rituals, therefore, play significant cultural and social roles; they help define us, remind us who we are, represent our values, and shape our behavior. By avoiding symbols and rituals the church opens the door for media and advertising to fill the void with consumer-driven values that are, for the most part, antithetical to Scripture.

How Are Christians to View
Symbols and Rituals?

Despite the prevalence of sacred symbols and spiritually formative rituals in Scripture and throughout the history of the church, Protestants tend to shy away from them. One pastor shared with me that he wanted to involve his congregation in responsive readings of Scripture but feared that his people would consider them "too liturgical or ritualistic." Another leader wanted to teach his congregation about the Christian tradition of crossing oneself after prayer as a way to signify the presence of the Trinity but was concerned his people would consider it "too Catholic." How should modern believers look at symbols and rituals?

Symbols and rituals play significant cultural and social roles; they help define us, remind us who we are, represent our values, and shape our behavior.

I want to stress that symbols are not objects of worship; I would never advocate worshiping material things. The best way to think of a sacred symbol or image is that it points to or stands in for something beyond itself. It's a visual aid or physical tool God can use to turn our attention to him, a window into divine reality, like a bridge to the spiritual realm. Sacred symbols, then, are more than merely symbolic, for they enable believers to move from the visible to the invisible world of spiritual reality. Symbols tend to be nonverbal; they utilize images that evoke emotion. Instead of an exclusively cognitive expression that minimizes the body and emotion, symbolic language fosters a spiritual experience that touches the whole person. People attach meaning to certain symbols and rituals that, by frequent use, deepen and increase in significance over time. But remember, the symbol is meaningful and significant only because we associate it with something or someone important to us. Communion, for example, is not just about the elements or how the rite is observed; it's about Jesus. Bread and wine are important only because they point us to our blessed Redeemer.

SACRAMENTALITY, WORSHIP, AND SPIRITUAL FORMATION

Symbols and rituals are part of a larger discussion on the topic of sacramentality, which has always been a contentious issue in the church. Christians have quarreled for centuries over what constitutes a sacrament and how many there are. Catholics recognize seven sacraments: baptism, confirmation, Eucharist, penance (or reconciliation), anointing of the sick, matrimony, and holy orders for service. Most Protestants recognize only baptism and Communion as sacraments, with some denominations referring to them instead as ordinances in an effort to distance themselves from the sacramental theology of Catholicism.

The main dispute over sacramentality centers on its function in public worship. Most contemporary Protestants have been taught that the sacraments (or ordinances) are nothing more than signs or symbols. Communion, for example, serves as a reminder of, or memorial to, Jesus' sacrifice on our behalf; the elements are a mere metaphor for Christ's body. Protestants may be surprised to learn that while the Reformation constituted, among other things, a rejection of Catholicism's abuse of the sacraments, the most prominent Reformers still held them in high regard. John Calvin, for example, believed that the sacraments are more than merely a sign or metaphor, that the physical things set forth in the sacraments lead us or direct us to spiritual things. Sacraments, therefore, play an active role in manifesting the reality they stand for.

Brief History of Sacramentality
in Gathered Worship

Churches of the New Testament had not yet developed a comprehensive theology of the sacraments, yet they operated with a sense of the sacred that was quite broad in its reach. As articulated later by medieval theologians Hugh of St. Victor and Thomas Aquinas, the early church considered any object or activity that mediated God's presence to humanity to be sacramental. The earliest believers were under no obligation to enumerate official church sacraments because they believed God was present with them at all times. The Son's incarnation—his taking on flesh and blood—convinced them that God could be found in our material world. The resurrection confirmed that Jesus is the true mediator of God's presence. While recognizing that God is always present everywhere in Jesus Christ through the power of the Holy Spirit, the first Christians also believed that the divine presence could be uniquely and intensely manifested in certain preordained objects and rituals. Word and Table, for example, were treated as sacred because they represented extraordinarily incomparable manifestations of God's presence. Even though early church leaders did not talk about sacraments per se, they attached what today we would call a sacramental sensibility to the powerful combination of Word and Table.

During the Middle Ages the balance of Word and Table began to shift in favor of the Eucharist, whose presentation became the climax of the worship service. Churchgoers, the majority of whom were uneducated, began to view the elements as endowed with magical powers to heal and bring good luck. Reformation leaders strongly opposed the Catholic Church's misappropriation of the sacraments, especially the Lord's Supper, and sought to return the church to its New Testament roots. Though well-intentioned, the Reformers' efforts to correct Catholicism's superstitious approach to the sacraments resulted in many Protestant denominations devaluing them, especially the Lord's Supper. In those churches the spotlight shifted away from Communion and focused instead on the sermon.

As ironic as it sounds the same Protestants who eschewed sacramentality in the Eucharist bestowed sacramental significance on the sermon, which became for them the high point—the meat and potatoes—of the service. Protestants encountered Christ most deeply through biblical preaching. Protestant worship effectively exchanged the embodied act of receiving Communion for the more cerebral, didactic experience of listening to a sermon. To this day many Protestants still emphasize preaching at the expense of the Lord's Supper by offering the latter monthly or quarterly and treating it as an afterthought haphazardly tacked on to the end of the sermon. Despite the Reformers' efforts to recover New Testament spirituality, many Protestant churches failed to capture the early church's powerful pairing of Word and Table as the Bible's most prominent means of encountering Christ whenever his followers assembled.

American frontier revivalism instigated yet another dramatic shift in sacramental theology. Charles Finney, influenced by Enlightenment thinking, did not regard the sacraments as a special manifestation of divine presence. Instead of realizing the presence of God in a sacred symbol or act, revivalists sought new measures to experience divine presence on a psychological and emotional level. Revival meetings attempted to create experiences in which God's presence could be felt or sensed. With the sign of God's presence having shifted from a sacred object to an objective experience, the ritual of coming forward to the anxious bench or making a decision for Christ took on a sacramental aura. Following the revivalists' lead, many churches began to treat the altar call as the climax of the service. Despite revivalism's many beneficial achievements, the movement unfortunately replaced the early church's dynamic duo of Word and Table with an act of human willpower—going forward, making a decision, saying a prayer—as the designated way to encounter Christ.

Inadequacy of contemporary worship music as a sacrament. While most Protestant churches continue to give preferential treatment to the sermon or the altar call, another element has emerged recently in various churches as a favored means of encountering Christ—contemporary worship music. This recent development has been heavily influenced by Pentecostal writers of the late twentieth century whose sacramental theology hinges on Psalm 22:3. The basic idea is that since God is enthroned on the praises of Israel, the heartfelt praise of God's people summons God's presence. Over the years this notion that praise music acts as the initial point of encounter with the divine presence has inspired many popular praise songs. Both the music and the philosophy it represents eventually found their way into non-mainline Protestant churches, causing many scholars (e.g., John Witvliet) to observe that worship music has taken on sacramental overtones in many churches today and become the ultimate means of encountering God.

It is not uncommon these days to hear Christians describe worship music as their "pathway to God" or to hear people insist that God showed up during the service when they heard their favorite worship song. I've heard numerous pastors proudly proclaim that their church's heavily music-driven worship services are designed to usher people "into the holy of holies" or take them on a "journey to God." Though such comments are well-intentioned, it is theologically incorrect to intimate that music leads us into God's presence. The writer of Hebrews clarifies that we enter "the Most Holy Place" only by the blood of Christ and that Jesus is the one who opens up for us the way to God (Hebrews 10:19-20). A certain song may cause someone to feel close to God, but it is through Jesus, and only Jesus, that we are truly drawn into fellowship with the Father.

I have been involved in church music ministry all my life. I admit that music can play a powerful role in worship and at times can point us to the Lord, but it is unrealistic to expect a worship tune, written in a pop style, to deliver an intimate, spiritually substantive encounter with Christ for everyone in the congregation every Sunday, no matter how well-crafted the song is. One drawback of treating music as a holy sacrament is that it is highly subjective. What if some in the pews don't like a particular song? What if they have difficulty identifying with the lyrics? What about those who don't even like music?

Music is emotional; by giving full expression to our joys as well as our sorrows, praise songs facilitate authentic worship. One of the dangers of projecting sacramental qualities onto music is that it could lead to emotional manipulation or cause us to depend on our favorite worship song to connect us to God instead of seeking Christ. Treating something as emotionally stimulating as music like it's a sacrament can plant seeds of doubt regarding the authenticity of one's spiritual experience. What if I'm not "feeling it" when that climactic song of the worship set is played? How do I know whether that transcendent impression of God I'm perceiving is from the Spirit or from the exhilarating crescendo reverberating from the electric guitar solo? Does an encounter with God have to be emotional to be valid?

Heavy emphasis on music can also cause us, if we're not careful, to sing about doing something and not actually do it. Singing is so much easier than doing; it's easier to sing about being committed to the Lord than to actually live for the Lord, easier to sing about being obedient than to actually obey. Singing about doing something or what we intend to do is not the same as actually following through with it; having sung it doesn't mean we've done it.

I don't deny that people can and do experience Jesus through worship music, but the medium has limits. Worship songs are wonderful vehicles for proclaiming who God is and celebrating what God has done, but it is unrealistic to expect music to play a sacramental role in gathered worship that is as consistently effective and universally applicable as the church's original vision of Word and Table.

Looking for the sacred in the wrong places. Our brief excursion into the history of sacramentalism reads as a tale of the good continually becoming the enemy of the best. In other words the New Testament's original positioning of Word and Table together as the primary means of encountering God was continually replaced by something good but ultimately inferior. Medieval churches focused on the Eucharist and minimized Scripture. Some Protestants swung the pendulum the other way and valued biblical preaching while diminishing the Lord's Supper. The revivalists preferred evangelistic preaching that climaxed with a gospel invitation or altar call. The late twentieth century introduced contemporary worship music, either in conjunction with the sermon or standing on its own merit, as yet another substitute for Word and Table. None of these historical developments is altogether bad. They all produced innovations that contributed significantly to communal worship. However, every time the church moved away from a sacramental perception of Word and Table together, our sense of the sacred became diminished, shrouded in superstition, or trivialized.

Nothing beats Word and Table. History also teaches that human beings, even evangelicals, hunger for sacramentality; we yearn for the sacred. We share a desire common among believers to experience God's presence during worship. Like other denominations and movements throughout history, we too continue to look for God in all the good, but not the best—meaning biblically mandated—places. In our defense the good is very good. On any given Sunday the sermon, altar call, or worship music can enable many churchgoers to connect with God. However, the weakness of such elements lies in the fact that they rely on human skill to work. We depend on the preacher to deliver a poignant sermon or a stirring altar call; we count on a group of gifted musicians to bring the worship set to a momentous climax.

The beauty of Word and Table is that in their most basic form they do not rely on human performance—either on the part of the leader or the congregation—to be effective. A simple reading of Scripture without comment can become an experience in which God, not the eloquence of the preacher, speaks to us. While a Communion song or devotional are effective segments in worship, the simple elements of bread and cup, prefaced by the traditional words of institution, are essentially all the invitation we need to fellowship with Jesus and his disciples around the Communion Table. The meaning lies in what the elements symbolize. Human performance is not a factor when it comes to Word and Table. All we have to do is show up and receive what God wants to give us— himself. Nothing beats Word and Table; it is the most dependable means of encountering our transcendent God.

SACRAMENTALITY FOR THE TWENTY-FIRST CENTURY

Historian James White suggests that today's church has entered "a new era in sacramental theology." White then submits Edward Schillebeeckx as a leading voice pointing in a new direction. Much of Schillebeeckx's theology, though, represents a return to the sacred sensibilities of the early church. Echoing the patristic writers, Schillebeeckx teaches that Jesus is the utmost "primordial sacrament." As the personal, intimate manifestation of divine grace, the Son of God provides the only means of access to the Father. The Bible teaches that no one comes to the Father except through the Son (John 14:6), that Jesus is the one who died in order to bring us to God (1 Peter 3:18). Only through Christ are we able to freely and confidently approach God (Ephesians 3:12). Sacraments are not things but encounters with the resurrected Christ made available to human beings through a visible form. Instituted by Christ himself, sacraments represent Jesus' promise—presented tangibly—to be present with and accessible to us.

Encountering Christ in the combination of Word and Table. Today many non-mainline Protestant churches are reinstating weekly Communion and in the process are rediscovering what the ancient church knew from firsthand experience—that Word and Table, alongside each other, serve as a powerful means of encountering Christ. The reason this combination is so spiritually potent is twofold. First, Word and Table effectively embody Christ. Jesus is the Word made flesh who dwells among us (John 1:14). The Word of God is not a book but a person. Christ speaks to us through the speaking and preaching of Scripture. Jesus is also the bread of life—whoever eats his flesh and drinks his blood has eternal life (John 6:35, 53-54). In the same way that Jesus fellowshipped with his disciples around a table, he meets us in the breaking of bread. Like the Emmaus travelers who recognized their risen Savior in the Scriptures and in the breaking of bread, modern churchgoers are finding and meeting Christ in a special way through Word and Table.

> *Sacraments are not things but encounters with the resurrected Christ made available to human beings through a visible form.*

Second, Word and Table offer two unique but complementary ways to experience Jesus. One is cerebral and didactic; the other is physical, holistic, and visceral. One is word-based, the other is visual. One involves hearing and listening; the other is action-oriented, summoning us to do something in response to what God has already done. One speaks generally to the head, the other to the heart. For example, the Word informs us about the promises of God, and the Table enables us to experience those promises tangibly, on a personal level; so what we know in our heads becomes embedded in our hearts. The promises of God are not something we merely intellectually consent to; they're an experiential reality we can affirm to the core of our being. The Table, therefore, offers many things that Word alone simply cannot accomplish.

Encountering Christ throughout a transforming worship service. I invite today's worship planners to rediscover the early church's sense of sacramentality. Even if we choose to steer clear of the word *sacrament*, we can rest assured that the Lord, who is never far from any one of us (Acts 17:27), can be encountered uniquely and powerfully during gathered worship. Though Word and Table represent a special manifestation of the presence of God in Christ, other parts of the service can also facilitate Christ's presence. Wherever and whenever two or three gather in Jesus' name, he promises to be there (Matthew 18:20). Blogger Michael Baggot posits that gathered worship offers sacramental realities that we can't get anywhere else; even if the service is bland and the minister is boring, those who come to church will "be rewarded with a divine encounter as real as those chronicled in Scripture." Worship's "sacramental realities" turn what appears from the outside to be an ordinary church service into a dynamic encounter with Jesus Christ. It is time for today's church to reclaim what the ancient church knew and what our friends in the High-Church tradition have always maintained—the unique ability of symbols and sacred acts to manifest God's presence is what differentiates gathered worship from a routine church meeting or activity.

Transforming worship recognizes the value of symbols and rituals for spiritual formation. Because they heighten our awareness of the divine presence, symbols and sacred acts can foster a transforming encounter with God. While there is nothing magical about them, sacred symbols and rituals hold great potential for encountering the transcendent, transforming presence of the triune God.

How Can You Foster a Sense of the Sacred in Your Setting?

Sacramentality has a sense of transcendence that inspires us to worship God with reverence and awe (Hebrews 12:28). At the same time it fosters intimacy with God, which reminds us that God is near and wants to be in relationship with us (Acts 17:27; Revelation 3:20).

Sacramentality, then, is both heavenly and down-to-earth at the same time; it conveys both God's transcendence (Isaiah 55:9) and his immanence (Matthew 1:23; John 1:14; Colossians 1:17; Hebrews 1:3). The challenge for those of us who plan and lead worship is to produce services that foster an encounter with the God who is far above and beyond us but at the same time actively involved in our world.

The longing for transcendence has led a growing number of churches to combine modern worship music with traditional liturgical elements. Sunday services in this vein feature contemporary-styled music—praise songs or short choruses—woven together with scripted prayers, responsive readings, and creeds that the congregation recites together. Since *liturgy* means "work of the people," liturgical services are by nature highly participatory, offering churchgoers more opportunities to engage in worship beyond merely singing. For example, the people are also invited to read Scripture together and pray. The biblical foundation of these time-honored liturgies ensures that Scripture will have a prominent place in the worship set. Liturgical prayers, being well-crafted as well as biblically based, also put words in the mouths of worshipers that are not only meaningful but also theologically sound.

As many churches have discovered, combining contemporary music and liturgical forms can be tricky, especially for churches with no prior experience with traditional liturgy. I've spoken with leaders who tried to introduce small, light doses of liturgy on Sunday morning but quickly abandoned it, claiming it didn't work for them. Contemporary Christian worship and liturgical practice represent two conflicting values that must be reconciled for the marriage to work. Christian music, much like secular entertainment, is built on the principle of innovation; something new or novel is valued because it keeps life from getting staid or boring. The beauty of liturgy is that, instead of being ephemeral and trendy, it is old, substantive, anchored in Christian tradition. Churches can rotate praise songs in and out and keep updating

their playlist to keep the music fresh and creative, but constantly introducing new liturgical elements every week reduces them to novelty
items and defeats their purpose. The value of liturgy lies in its famil-
iarity. Everyone can join in prayer or a reading because they know it;
they've heard it repeated over and over every Sunday. Instead of
changing with the times, liturgy, by its very nature, is enduring, it pos-
sesses staying power. Words and melodies heard weekly at church can
remain with us for the rest of our lives, bringing comfort in difficult
seasons and giving us words to pray when we've run out of our own
words. People want to participate in the liturgy because the words have
become meaningful to them.

To maximize the potential of a liturgical element, I recommend
making it a regular feature of gathered worship, even if it's for a season.
Whether it's a specific moment of the service like a call to worship or
benediction or a specific element like the Apostles' Creed or Lord's
Prayer, make it a regular occurrence—weekly or monthly—so it can
become embedded in the hearts and minds of the congregation.
Weaving liturgical elements into contemporary worship can result in a
rich spiritual experience for God's people.

This chapter has been aimed primarily at nonliturgical churches, but
I do have a suggestion for liturgical churches and those from a High-
Church tradition: make sure the meaning of sacred symbols and acts
doesn't get lost during the service. Growing up Lutheran, I didn't learn
the meaning of certain symbols or the reason behind the rituals until
later in life. I remember my first confirmation class when the pastor
showed up in civilian clothes instead of his usual Sunday vestments. It
was mildly traumatic for a twelve-year-old, like seeing your first-grade
teacher at the grocery store and realizing that she didn't spend every
waking hour of her life in school, that she had a life outside the classroom.
When someone explained why our pastor wore different clothes for
worship services, I was able to grasp the significance of his Sunday attire.

Explaining periodically the meaning behind a symbol or the biblical precedence for a ritual enhances your congregation's understanding and deepens their experience of it. Don't assume they know, and those that do know will benefit by being reminded. Take thirty seconds to expound on a line in the liturgy. After, your people will say it or pray it with renewed vigor. Symbols, sacraments, and liturgy lose their sense of transcendence and become mere religious artifacts and empty rituals if worshipers don't appreciate their value.

Churches have varying degrees of ritual. They all have set routines or an activity they do every week that is unique or distinctive. At one church where I served, we all stood after the offering and sang—the same song every week—celebrating our unity in Christ; that was our thing. Whether you're high church, low church, or somewhere in-between, now would be a good time to evaluate the rituals your church has established in worship—those things you do every Sunday. Are they still effective? Are they substantive? Do they accomplish what needs to be accomplished? How can they be more effective? Is it time to introduce a song, prayer, spoken response, or some other routine that would enable your services to be more spiritually formative? If so, what might that be? Make sure all facets of the service contribute something substantive to a formative, transcendent worship experience.

Part 2

DISTINCTIVE ELEMENTS OF TRANSFORMING WORSHIP

❦

OVER THE NEXT FIVE CHAPTERS, we will investigate five distinctive elements of a transforming worship service: prayer, Scripture reading, confession, the Lord's Supper, and baptism. I will approach each of these worship components sacramentally—as routines and rituals rooted in Christian tradition, sometimes utilizing symbols and gestures, that facilitate life-changing encounters with the living Christ. My goal is that we will be more intentional with these service elements in regard to spiritual formation, that we view these corporate practices as vital to the spiritual life, and that we, as worship planners and leaders, unleash their full potential to transform lives.

6

LET US PRAY!

❦

T HE STORY OF JESUS' cleansing the temple catches the one who preached peace and love in a rare act of violent aggression. As the Gospels report (Matthew 21:12-13; Mark 11:15-26), Jesus drove the merchants out of the temple courtyard, sent their customers home, and overturned the tables of the money changers. Many have difficulty imagining gentle Jesus flexing his muscles with such brute force. Why the rude behavior? What incited this sudden outburst of anger from the Son of God? In one word, it was abuse. The money changers were taking advantage of the poor by overcharging them. Thus they were robbing people under the pretense of religious service. Equally serious was the injustice done to the Lord, for blatant commercialism had turned the temple into a noisy marketplace, a far cry from the true business God intended for his house: prayer. It didn't matter that the commerce was for religious purposes; Christ was adamant that his Father's house was a place where prayer is paramount. Jesus' most militant act of civil disobedience was not only in reaction to the maltreatment of the poor but also in response to the devaluation of prayer in gathered worship.

Do We Pray Together?

I often wonder whether the place that prayer occupies in modern worship matches the high priority Jesus gave it. I suspect not, for, unfortunately, the majority of the services I've participated in allowed more time for announcements than for prayer. Granted, many of the worship songs we sing are prayers, but how many congregation members pray as they sing? Should singing our prayers completely replace speaking them? Do sung prayers allow the congregation to articulate specific prayer requests? Do they offer worshipers the opportunity to intercede on behalf of their community, the church, or the world? Do we indeed pray when we gather?

Another question to consider is whether or not we, the people, get to pray during worship. I've sat through many church services where the pastor or worship leader was the only one who prayed. Congregants were expected to pray along in agreement with the leader's prayers. And all God's people said "Amen" on cue. But those of us sitting in the pews never uttered a word of prayer the entire service. When I hear a pastor say, "Let us pray," I often want to blurt out, "Yes! Please! Let *us* pray!"

How can we expect worshipers to truly encounter God during Sunday services if we don't give them a chance to talk directly to the Lord? Not letting the people pray inadvertently communicates that prayer is something that only professional clergy are either allowed to do or are capable of doing. As a result, we have a growing number of Christians who claim to believe in the power of prayer but seldom pray.

Corporate Prayer in the Early Church

The book of Acts portrays the first Christians as passionately devoted to prayer (Acts 2:42) and features them praying together every time they gathered. The church at Antioch regularly fasted and prayed (Acts 13:1-3). Following Jewish custom that set aside three times a day for prayer, Peter, John, and several other disciples headed to the temple at the appointed hour to pray together (Acts 3:1). Psalm 55:17 confirms that our Hebrew ancestors were committed to praying when they awoke, at midday, and at night before they went to bed. Historian Aaron Milavec substantiates that this Jewish prayer regimen carried over into early Christian worship, but this does not necessarily mean that the entire community gathered three times a day; instead, those working in the same shop or living in the same household would meet at pre-determined hours to pray together. The first Christians were devoted to prayer—especially communal prayer.

> *How can we expect worshipers to truly encounter God during Sunday services if we don't give them a chance to talk directly to the Lord?*

Alan Kreider observes that Christianity's earliest thinkers wrote more extensively on prayer than on the sermon; their goal was to offer practical guidance regarding corporate prayer, which they considered to be the power center of their gatherings. When they prayed together, the early Christians were convinced they were engaging in spiritual battle. Clement of Alexandria, writing in the second century, describes the church as an "army without weapons" composed of people from all walks of life waging spiritual warfare against sickness and the evil forces of this world. Origen believed prayer to be a source of unlimited power, a weapon more powerful than military might. The church originated as an army of prayer warriors who believed prayer changes things.

First-century Christians took prayer seriously. Justin Martyr depicts worshipers at his church in Rome as praying earnestly. Ancient Christians typically prayed standing with eyes open and arms raised heavenward; their outspread hands represented innocence, imitated Jesus on the cross, and communicated their readiness to face persecution or torture for their faith. In his treatise on prayer, Origen allowed those with physical ailments to sit, but he insisted that everyone else extend their hands and elevate their eyes; early Christians were taught that this was the physical posture that enabled their souls to pray most effectively. Some ancient church leaders also encouraged worshipers to pray aloud simultaneously. Early believers prayed mightily, vigorously, and were highly expressive to the point of groaning or crying out loud. Kreider describes their prayers as "gutsy" and "passionate" because they emerged from the everyday struggles and concerns of people who had little control over what happened to them in their lives. Prayers spoken at church empowered them to face life's challenges.

Let's examine in greater detail the nature and content of the prayers in early church services. Biblical and historical accounts disclose that the petitions offered by our Christian ancestors were participatory, intercessory in nature, filled with gratitude, and included both spontaneous and scripted prayers.

All in. When describing the church at prayer, Luke frequently uses the word *all*, suggesting that their intercessions were highly participatory. We are told early on that the apostles and the women "*all* joined together constantly in prayer" (Acts 1:14). When Paul huddled with the elders from the church at Ephesus, "he knelt down with *all of them* and prayed" (Acts 20:36). When Luke and Paul departed from Tyre on their way to Jerusalem, the entire church gathered to see them off; "*all of them*, including wives and children," knelt to pray right there on the beach (Acts 21:5). In each of these examples, we do not get the impression that prayer was a solo act in which only the leader spoke. "They raised their voices together" (Acts 4:24) because of their shared commitment to prayer. Robert Webber insists that there was no such thing as pastoral prayer in the ancient church, for prayer "belonged to the people and arose out of the congregation." The church in the post–New Testament era was a place where everyone felt free to participate during prayer. The church did not start with separate prayer ministries involving a handful of faithful members who met in a secluded basement every Wednesday night. Instead, Christians prayed every time they gathered and it was a group effort.

Praying for others. Scripture indicates that the early church spent a great deal of time praying for one another. Paul exhorted the church at Ephesus to always pray for God's people (Ephesians 6:18). Paul and those first Christian worshipers were merely following the example set by Jesus, who, when he lived among them, prayed predominantly on behalf of others, especially his followers. The night he was betrayed, Jesus spent significant time beseeching his heavenly Father to protect his followers, unify them, and sanctify them; he also prayed for those who would eventually come to faith—Christians down through the ages (John 17:11, 17, 20-21). Jesus' prayers were not confined to his circle of disciples. While hanging on the cross, for example, he interceded for those responsible for his suffering, including those who tortured him (Luke 23:34). Intercessory prayer became the lifeblood of the church because it was the backbone of Jesus' own prayer life and because it is one of the main functions of the priesthood of believers (1 Peter 2:5, 9). According to Hughes Oliphant Old, the major prayer of the service for the first four centuries of church history and during the Reformation was a prayer specifically devoted to intercession.

The Pauline Epistles reveal that the most prominent petition on the minds of early church leaders was for spiritual growth and maturity among congregation members. The New Testament church interceded faithfully on behalf of those in need, with special attention given to fellow believers and their spiritual formation. The prayers of those initial Christians, however, were far from parochial. Writing to his young protégé, Pastor Timothy, Paul urges that "petitions, prayers, intercession and thanksgiving be made for all people" (1 Timothy 2:1). Our spiritual ancestors not only interceded for the needs of their community; they prayed regularly for those outside their circle as well. Paul specified that petitions be raised on behalf of kings and all authority figures so that

God's people would be able to live quiet and peaceful lives (1 Timothy 2:2). They were to pray for government rulers and civic leaders—those who, by their policies and actions, directly influenced everyone's welfare, including the Christians' efforts to live out their faith. The New Testament's vision of corporate prayer goes beyond the immediate needs of the congregation to address concerns in the broader society as well as social and political issues throughout their world.

The church in its early stages remained steadfast in its devotion to intercessory prayer. Tertullian reports that the churches at Carthage, in the African province of the Roman Empire, prayed regularly for the emperor and for peace to prevail. By the fourth century most churches had developed a set prayer list for worship, and though the list differed from church to church, it represented the church's attempt to follow Jesus' example and Paul's explicit directions to pray for others. Early Christian gatherings typically featured a prayer for the worldwide church—the body of Christ as well as the ministries of their local congregation. The service included prayers for church leaders—the bishop, presbyters, and deacons—as well as separate petitions for those in need, such as widows, orphans, prisoners, the oppressed, the sick, and the poor. They also prayed for the emperor, the king, the governor, and their local magistrates. The ancient church was a distinctly prayerful enterprise in which everyone actively interceded before the Lord on behalf of family, friends, the church, government leaders, and the world at large.

Steeped in gratitude. New Testament writers were adamant that Christians convey gratefulness to God. Paul instructed the church at Philippi to offer prayers and petitions "with thanksgiving" (Philippians 4:6) and instructed the Thessalonians to "give thanks in all circumstances" (1 Thessalonians 5:18). He advised the Ephesian church to speak to one another in psalms, hymns, and spiritual songs while "always giving thanks to God the Father for everything" (Ephesians 5:20). The Colossians were urged to do everything in Jesus' name, "giving thanks to God the Father through him" (Colossians 3:17). Paul repeatedly taught believers to express gratitude whenever they prayed together.

Though many regard praise and thanksgiving as synonymous, Old distinguishes the two: *praise* is our response to the awe-inspiring presence of God, while *thanksgiving* is the recognition that God has blessed us. Throughout the Old Testament, especially the Psalms, the Hebrew verb *barak* is usually translated "bless," but the original meaning connotes the idea of thanksgiving. We bless God because he first blessed us. God blesses human beings by imparting good things to us; we in return bless God by praising him for his goodness toward us. We bless God out of gratitude for all he has done for us. In keeping with their Hebrew heritage, the first Christians made prayers of thanksgiving a vital part of their gatherings.

> *The ancient church was a distinctly prayerful enterprise in which everyone actively interceded before the Lord on behalf of family, friends, the church, government leaders, and the world at large.*

Scripted and spontaneous. There's a bit of controversy today as to which is more appropriate for gathered worship—scripted or spontaneous prayer. Liturgical churches favor prewritten prayers while contemporary congregations lean toward spontaneity—each side believing, of course, that their practice is more spiritual than the other. Modern churchgoers may be surprised to learn that early church practice featured both scripted and spontaneous prayers.

By the Book. Scripture discloses that the first Christians, most of whom were Jewish, remained committed to "the prayers" (Acts 2:42 ESV), which, for the most part, refers to the traditional prayers of their Hebrew faith. These would include prayers of thanksgiving, blessing, benediction, and the Psalms, which occupied a major place in early Christian worship (see

Ephesians 5:19; Colossians 3:16). Pious Jews would have memorized these prayers (and all the psalms) so they could participate actively when fellow believers gathered to pray.

In this same spirit the early believers prayed the Lord's Prayer. The first-century document known as the *Didache* reveals that the New Testament church held in high regard the prayer Jesus taught his disciples. Christianity's earliest worshipers regarded the Lord's Prayer as a divine gift delivered to them by Christ himself. The extensive use of plural pronouns throughout the Lord's Prayer suggests that Jesus intended his followers to recite it publicly. For that reason the *Didache* recommends that Christians recite it three times a day, presumably as part of their daily prayer regimen.

Interestingly, the *Didache* also warns against praying in a perfunctory manner like "the hypocrites" and then proceeds to suggest reciting the Lord's Prayer as a way to avoid praying hypocritically. So even though the early church prayed this familiar prayer regularly, they were to pray it sincerely, like they meant what they were saying. The first Christians, therefore, found it meaningful to pray liturgically, using old, prewritten prayers borrowed from their Hebrew heritage combined with new Christian expressions, such as the Lord's Prayer.

Free to improvise. In addition to praying formal, scripted prayers, the first followers of Christ also gathered in homes for informal times of prayer (see Acts 4:23-26; 12:5, 12). The tiny band of disciples prayed for discernment in appointing a leader to replace Judas (Acts 1:24), for boldness in proclaiming the gospel (Acts 4:23-31), and for Peter when he was in prison (Acts 12:5, 12). Each of these circumstances suggests a more spontaneous approach to gathered prayer—something which came quite naturally for history's first messianic Jews. Spontaneity was intrinsic to the Jewish prayer experience. Rabbis were known for encouraging spontaneous expression even for fixed prayers; the thought here was that if people couldn't bring something new to their regular petitions, they prayed in vain. The freedom to improvise prevented their liturgy from becoming rigid and boring.

Spontaneity was also achieved by using the liturgy or Scripture as a springboard for prayer. Acts 4:24-30, for example, presents one of the first recorded prayers of the church, and it begins with praise straight out of Psalm 146:6: "Sovereign Lord, you made the heavens and the earth and the sea, and everything in them." The next part, Acts 4:25-26, is lifted from Psalm 2:

> Why do the nations rage
> and the peoples plot in vain?
> The kings of the earth rise up
> and the rulers band together
> against the Lord
> and against his anointed one.

At this point, the prayer goes off-script. Instead of continuing to string together fragments from the Psalms, it applies the ones already quoted to Christ: "Herod and Pontius Pilate met together with the Gentiles and the people of Israel in this city to conspire against your holy servant Jesus, whom you anointed" (Acts 4:27). The prayer closes by beseeching the Lord to enable the church to proclaim the gospel in the face of opposition and for the Lord to heal and perform miracles in Jesus' name (Acts 4:29-30). What began as a well-worn psalm reading quickly turned into a passionate plea centered on the urgent needs of the moment.

The Lord's Prayer was often utilized in the early church in a similar, free-flowing manner. Considering that the *Didache* urged believers to gather three times a day to pray the Lord's Prayer, it is unlikely that they met for the thirty seconds it takes to recite it and then went their separate ways. Instead, the Lord's Prayer provided a framework for intercession; Christians expounded extemporaneously on the prayer to fit the circumstances of the moment and the needs of those who were present. Like the psalms, the Lord's Prayer allowed worshipers to add their concerns and personal requests to the prayers of the community. Even though the early church prayed liturgically, they weren't rigidly bound to it but were free to ad-lib. Their flexibility with all prewritten forms breathed fresh vitality into the church's ministry of intercession.

Room for both types of prayer. Since the New Testament church valued and practiced both scripted and spontaneous prayer, it is time for modern Christians to rethink their biases against either approach. Some prefer scripted prayer because it feels safe and orderly. Going off-script is risky to them, even threatening. But if it's led well, spontaneous prayer can be prevented from getting out of hand. Having led numerous prayer groups, I have had to step in at times to remind people not to be long-winded or gossip in the guise of prayer or pray manipulatively or push a political agenda. Establishing clear guidelines is not only a preventative measure, it assures those who are uneasy with the idea that spontaneous prayer does not have to turn into a free-for-all.

Some who champion spontaneous prayer believe it to be more Spirit-led than scripted prayer. Constance Cherry argues that the Holy Spirit is always at work before, during, and after a service. "Though the Holy Spirit may appear to us to act spontaneously, this is because we are often unaware of the Spirit's action until it occurs, for we are not often privy to God's actions in advance." It is presumptuous, therefore, to conclude that the Spirit operates most effectively or exclusively in a spontaneous fashion. A prayer crafted ahead of time can be just as anointed as one spoken at the moment.

Those who gravitate toward spontaneous prayer also tend to be suspicious of scripted or liturgical prayer, which they regard as stiff, rigid, and inauthentic. For them, saying the Lord's Prayer every week constitutes vain repetition. But as those first Christians demonstrated, it is possible to pray an old, familiar prayer like we mean it. Even though the words are the same every time we pray, we can still engage with prayers that are tried and true because our circumstances will be different each time we pray.

Each of the two types of prayer brings something unique to gathered worship. Prewritten prayers, especially liturgical compositions from the great prayer books and hymnals, are typically more formal, employ exalted language, and remind us that we are in the presence of a holy, majestic God. Improvised prayers, on the other hand, tend to be more informal, conversational, use common language, and help us remember that God is near and working actively in our lives and throughout the world. Scripted prayer captures God's transcendence while spontaneous prayer realizes God's immanence.

LEARNING HOW TO PRAY AT CHURCH

When the disciples asked Jesus to teach them how to pray, their teacher didn't launch into a three-point sermon. He simply prayed and invited them into the experience of conversing intimately with his heavenly Father. Jesus knew that prayer is not something we learn from a textbook. We learn how to pray by doing it. By the same token, New Testament believers did not need prayer workshops or books on the topic. They learned how to pray at church. The psalm readings and traditional Hebrew prayers modeled for them how to talk to God. Listening to the spontaneous intercessions voiced every week taught them the importance of praying not only for their own needs but also for the cares and concerns of others. The church depicted in the book of Acts did not have to be convinced that prayer was powerful; they experienced it as such every time they gathered.

Foundational to any biblical theology of gathered prayer is the concept of the royal priesthood of Christ. The book of Hebrews proclaims that Jesus Christ is our great high priest who has ascended into heaven and that one of his priestly roles is intercessory prayer

(Hebrews 4:14). In the same way that the high priest in the Old Testament entered into God's presence to represent his people, Jesus Christ entered heaven to intercede for us. Unlike Israel's high priest who on the Day of Atonement offered a sacrifice and entered the holy of holies alone while the people waited outside, Jesus, having made the ultimate sacrifice, takes us with him into God's presence. He presents us to the Father as holy and sanctified (2 Corinthians 4:14; Hebrews 10:10).

Jesus' ongoing ministry of intercession. The author of Hebrews assures us that prayer is not some dutiful obligation that Jesus sometimes dabbles in but that Christ "always lives" to intercede for us (Hebrews 7:25). When it comes to intercessory prayer, Jesus is "always on the job" as *The Message* quaintly puts it. Paul affirms that the resurrected Christ actively prays for us (Romans 8:34). At this moment Jesus is upholding you and me in prayer, interceding relentlessly and passionately on our behalf.

We learn how to pray by doing it.

Because the Son of God took on human form and dwelled among us, he intercedes as one who understands what it is like to be human; he can empathize with our weaknesses (Hebrews 4:15). Jesus' intercessions for us are tenderly sympathetic and compassionate. He knows what it's like to suffer because he suffered harrowing abuse at the hands of his executioners. Jesus is not indifferent to our pain and sorrow; he empathizes as one who himself suffered.

Jesus sanctifies our prayers. Our avid, heavenly intercessor sanctifies our prayers. James Torrance asserts that "Jesus takes our prayers—our feeble, selfish, inarticulate prayers—he cleanses them, makes them his prayers." Jesus stands in the gap between human beings and God as our great high priest offering to God the prayer and worship we are incapable of offering due to our sinfulness. When we pray in Jesus' name, it is not some mindless catch phrase tacked on to the end of the prayer. As

Torrance explains, we pray in Jesus' name because he is offering up prayers in our name, for our sake:

> We can only pray in the name of Christ because Christ has already in our name, offered up our desires to God and continues to offer them. In our name he lived a life in the Spirit agreeable to the will of God. In our name and in our place he vicariously confessed our sins and submitted for us to the verdict of guilty on the cross, taking the condemnation of our sins to himself . . . and in our name gave thanks to God. We pray in the name of Christ because of what Christ has already done for us, and is doing for us today in our name, on our behalf.

Prayer is effective not because of our righteousness or pious eloquence, but because Jesus Christ takes up our cause and intercedes for us (1 John 2:1).

Paul admits the sobering reality that in our human weakness we do not know how to pray (Romans 8:26). Prayer is not something we do in our power but something God initiates and invites us into. Our job is to cooperate with Jesus in prayer, trusting him to pray for us, with us, and in us. Cooperating with Christ in prayer removes the pressure to perform that we sometimes feel, especially when praying with others. We can let go of our fear of praying incorrectly. We don't have to let our fear of saying the wrong thing prevent us from praying. Jesus will take whatever we say, no matter how simple, scattered, or inept it seems to us and will make it right.

Continuing Jesus' ministry of intercessory prayer. Jesus invites his church to join him in his ongoing ministry of intercession. Corporate prayer puts us in touch with the needs of others. Instead of retreating from the world, we become more engaged with it. Dirk Lange insists that corporate prayer opens the windows and doors of our church buildings and enables us to hear the cries of our neighbors.

Whenever Christians assemble, we become a royal priesthood, praying in partnership with our risen Savior, our prayers echoing his. This priestly calling pertains to the entire community, not just the professional clergy. Every time we pray together, we fulfill our mission and calling as Christ's intercessors for the world.

TEACH US HOW TO PRAY TOGETHER, JESUS!

An old Latin phrase captures the formative nature of gathered prayer: *lex orandi, lex credendi, lex vivendi.* The line conveys the idea that the way we pray informs our beliefs, which in turn transforms how we live. If the way we pray affects the way we live, we must never stop growing in our understanding and experience of prayer. Twenty-first-century churchgoers can learn how to pray the same way Jesus' first disciples learned—by praying with Jesus, who is present among us every Sunday when we gather together. Congregational prayer teaches new believers, for example, how to converse with God and demonstrates to unbelievers that prayer is a natural part of the Christian life. Furthermore, not everyone is comfortable praying out loud or in a group. Congregational prayer helps timid members become more willing and able to pray aloud by providing a safe, familiar setting to practice praying.

> *Every time we pray together, we fulfill our mission and calling as Christ's intercessors for the world.*

Gathered prayer is not only educational for those new in the faith; veteran prayer warriors benefit as well. When the disciples requested that Jesus teach them to pray, they were not novices at any of the spiritual disciplines. Prayer was an essential element of their Jewish heritage. Yet the intimacy with which the Son of God addressed the Father and the depth of his prayers made Jesus' followers realize they still had much to learn. In the same way, longtime Christians can find fresh words to integrate into their prayer lives and gain new perspectives by joining in the intercessions of their church family. When it comes to prayer, there is always more to learn.

How to Develop a More Formative Approach to Prayer in Your Setting

Our job as worship planners and leaders, according to Zac Hicks, is not only to facilitate prayer on Sunday but also to train Christians to pray Monday through Saturday. To that end, the New Testament model for gathered prayer offers three valuable suggestions for today's leaders to consider.

Let the people pray. Give your congregation ample opportunity to participate in prayer. Include prayers that the people can say together, reading the words off a front screen or from their bulletins. I've been in small, intimate churches where the congregation called out prayer requests or wrote them down. While that may not be practical in large churches, it is possible to create a participatory prayer experience in a large congregation. I've had good results by inviting worshipers to gather in groups of four or five with those seated around them, listing on a screen specific needs in our community and in the world, and then letting the groups pray together over those needs as they are led. Don't let the fact that your congregation is large prevent you from enabling your people to fulfill their collective calling as a priesthood of believers. For the benefit of seekers, explain briefly why Christians pray, invite them to join in, but give them the option of not participating and quietly observing if they're not comfortable praying. Give introverts an out as well. If someone isn't comfortable praying aloud or in a group, encourage them to pray silently by themselves. It's time to dispel the notion that religious professionals are the only ones qualified to pray; it is time to return prayer to the people and provide opportunities for them to pray together.

Include prayers of intercession and thanksgiving. For guidance on what exactly to pray, follow the example set by the New Testament church and pray for the Holy Spirit to help your people grow in the faith and knowledge of Christ, hold fast to sound doctrine, develop godly character, and grow in their love for one another. Have your congregation pray as Jesus did for the coming of God's kingdom (Matthew 6:10) as well as for the spreading of the gospel, the building up of the church, and the reforming of society. Intercede faithfully for those suffering persecution or discrimination for the sake of the gospel—Christians who are oppressed, falsely accused, imprisoned, kidnapped, raped, and tortured because of their faith. Be sure to give thanks to the Lord often during worship (1 Timothy 2:1). Wise leaders establish a balanced prayer life for their congregants by offering them the opportunity to participate in Christ's ongoing ministry of intercession and express gratitude regularly to God.

Be open to both scripted and spontaneous prayers. We observed that the New Testament church practiced two different forms of corporate prayer: scripted and spontaneous. Scot McKnight commends both: pray spontaneously from the heart but also pray the prayers of the Bible, the psalms, and those of the traditional church found in prayer books and hymnals. To ensure a healthy mix of both, pastors and worship leaders must expose their congregations to the great prayers of the church and at the same time teach their people how to engage in spontaneous communal prayer. If either of those approaches to prayer is new for your congregation, introduce them slowly and incrementally, explaining the biblical support cited earlier in this chapter.

If your church is not accustomed to liturgical prayer, begin with something simple, like the Lord's Prayer. Don't do it occasionally, like it's a novelty item; do it often, regularly, every week. The beauty of liturgical prayer is that the repetition enables the prayer to become familiar, so the community is more apt to participate because they know it. If you're convinced that a number of your attendees will balk when they hear the word *liturgy*, downplay the liturgical aspects of the prayer. After all, most liturgical prayers are based on Scripture or are actual Bible passages read verbatim. Emphasize the fact that you're praying Scripture, not that you're making them pray liturgically. As time goes on, expose congregants to some of the substantive prayers found in the great hymnals and prayer books.

If spontaneous prayer is a new idea for your church, start with the basics. For example, have the congregation pray individually and silently for sixty seconds before inviting them to pray en masse or in groups. When you sense they're ready to pray spontaneously out loud, give clear directions, and, again, allow seekers to observe if they're not comfortable participating. If you're concerned about things getting out of hand, offer a few simple guidelines at the beginning (e.g., don't be long-winded, don't gossip, etc.). Allowing your congregation to pray together will interject fresh energy and vitality into your services.

I believe that God is calling today's church to once again become a place where God's people learn how to pray. It is time to embrace fully our calling to be a praying presence in the world, to pray fervently for one another and for the world. May the Lord find us on our knees faithfully interceding for those in the church—our friends and families—as well as those outside the church—our neighbors, coworkers, classmates, as well as those who are suffering or in need.

7

Engaging the Preached and Unpreached Word of God

꧁꧂

I n the Old Testament, Ezekiel reminisces about his commissioning ceremony as a prophet during which he was required to physically eat the scroll containing the Hebrew Scriptures (Ezekiel 3:1-3). This rather peculiar initiation rite illustrates that the Word of God is meant to be ingested into our very being so it becomes a flesh-and-blood reality in our lives rather than mere words on a piece of parchment. When we eat, the food is digested and turned into the cells and tissues comprising our physical bodies. By the same token, when we take in God's Word and let it shape our innermost being—when we "eat the book," so to speak—we turn into a certain kind of person. In the same way that food forms us physically, God's Word can form us into complete human beings.

Jesus affirms that the path to discipleship involves remaining faithful to or continuing in his teaching (John 8:31). Spiritual formation cannot occur without regular exposure to and adherence to the Word of God. For that reason Scripture figures prominently in a transforming worship service. Most modern churchgoers view the sermon as the time in the service devoted to the Word of God. As important as the sermon is, it is not the only effective means of communicating Scripture in a potentially edifying manner. Throughout history the public reading of God's Word has played a uniquely formative role in the lives of believers.

PUBLIC READING OF SCRIPTURE
IN THE JEWISH TRADITION

The Bible presents numerous examples of God's people gathering specifically to hear their leaders read aloud the Word of God. Moses shared with the Hebrews all that God spoke to him atop Mount Sinai (Exodus 24:3). During a covenant renewal service, Joshua was scrupulously careful not to leave out a single word while reading the Book of the Law to the entire assembly of Israel, including all the women and children, and even the foreigners who lived among them (Joshua 8:34-35). King Josiah summoned his people together, read the Book of the Covenant to them, committed himself to follow God's commandments, then invited his people to dedicate their lives to the Lord (2 Kings 23:1-3). After the Jewish exiles rebuilt the walls of Jerusalem, Ezra read to them the Book of the Law from daybreak until noon while the people listened attentively; the Levites explained the meaning of God's Word so everyone could understand it (Nehemiah 8:1-8). Each of these examples features the public reading of God's Word to edify all who heard it. In almost every case Scripture is reportedly read without commentary, the lone exception being the Levites interpreting for Ezra while he read. The emphasis, therefore, is not on preaching but on the simple reading of God's Word—letting Scripture stand on its own strength.

In the same way that food forms us physically, God's Word can form us into complete human beings.

Because of these Old Testament examples, Israel eventually made Scripture reading a mainstay in its worship services. By the first century it was customary for pious Jews to meet at local synagogues on the

Sabbath, read passages from their Hebrew Scriptures, and have someone briefly comment on them. Luke describes a time when Jesus entered the synagogue in his hometown of Nazareth, as he typically did every Sabbath, but on this occasion Jesus stood up, read from the prophet Isaiah, and explained to everyone that the words they just heard were being fulfilled right before their very eyes in him (Luke 4:15-22).

PUBLIC READING OF SCRIPTURE IN
THE FIRST-CENTURY CHURCH

The habitual reading of Scripture, having already become one of the main activities of the synagogue, quickly became the normative practice for Christian worship. The apostle Paul directs Timothy, a young leader in the church, to devote significant time and energy to the public reading of Scripture as a prelude to exhortation and teaching (1 Timothy 4:13). As far as Paul is concerned, one of the principal reasons Christians assemble in the first place is to read Scripture together.

Justin Martyr reports that first-century Christians living in the cities, as well as those out in the country, gathered together every Sunday to read "the memoirs of the apostles" as well as the writings of the Old Testament prophets, after which the presiding leader would offer verbal instruction and exhortation. The public reading of Scripture, therefore, is a longstanding tradition in the church.

A church leader standing in front of the congregation and reading passages from the Bible conjures up for many of us an image of someone droning on in a flat, monotone voice, with little or no facial expression. Those of us who grew up going to church have endured our fair share of lethargic Scripture readings. However, the public reading of Scripture in the early church was far from drab and boring.

Oral-aural culture. To appreciate fully what those nascent church readings were like, we have to understand the unique role of the spoken word in ancient culture. Today, we live in a print culture; nearly everyone can read, most Christians own a Bible, if not several of them. Before the printing press, believers experienced God's Word not through private, silent reading but as a verbal, public presentation. Christianity itself was birthed into a distinctively oral-aural culture, which was characterized by a dynamic interplay between speaking and hearing.

In the first century the majority of the population was illiterate. It is estimated that only 5 percent of the populous could read or write and those were mostly the affluent, elite members of society. Very few had access to any sacred writings. Everything people learned came from someone they knew; everything they knew was by word of mouth. Paul's observation, in Romans 10:17, that people come to faith as a result of hearing God's message, illustrates that ancient believers learned about Christ by hearing Scripture read to them. The public reading of Scripture, therefore, played a significant role in the spiritual lives of the early Christians.

The implications of an oral-aural environment are far-reaching. First, it meant that the written word was subservient to the spoken word. Anything written would have to be copied by hand multiple times because there was no way to mass-produce it. So verbal or oral communication took center stage, so to speak, and was considered true communication. What we would conceive as a book was merely a bunch of words waiting to be spoken and communicated. The written word was merely a script intended to be performed before an audience. The earliest Christian authors wrote their inspired works anticipating they would be shared publicly. Paul instructed that his letters be read aloud whenever Christians gathered (Colossians 4:16; 1 Thessalonians 5:27). In the New Testament world, the spoken word trumped the written word.

Performance mentality. An oral-aural culture also demanded that reading Scripture should take on somewhat of a performance mentality. We today have an aversion to performance in worship. We often associate performing with acting, which seems inauthentic and therefore

inappropriate for worship. To capture the spirit of New Testament
church readings, think in terms of effective communication rather than
inauthentic playacting. Written pieces were read or performed skillfully,
with passion, to be communicated effectively.

In ancient times public readers were expected to demonstrate prodi-
gious communication skills. Someone who could speak well could go
far in the ancient Mediterranean world. Paul, unfortunately, was not
known as a strong orator. His letters were reputed to be weighty, strong,
and forceful, but his physical presence was weak and unimpressive; his
speaking abilities didn't amount to much at all (2 Corinthians 10:10).
Public readers, on the other hand, were known as riveting storytellers.
They were good at impersonation and establishing rapport with an audience; they could portray characters and express emotion. In other
words, early church Scripture readings were far from being perfunctory,
lackadaisical recitations but were instead lively, dynamic, passionate
presentations. First-century Christians went to church expecting to hear
the acclaimed stories about Jesus, the apostolic letters, and the Old Testament writings enacted, embodied, and re-presented in fresh and
exciting ways.

As far as what these ancient, Bible-reading "performances" were like,
it is important to note that Scripture was most often read in its entirety
in those days. Instead of excerpts, entire books or letters were read in
one sitting. If you heard only a portion of the writings and not the whole
thing, you'd be missing something and wouldn't be able to understand
it. Even more astounding to imagine is that these unabridged versions
of Scripture were most often delivered from memory. All the New Testament writings are short enough to be memorized and that's what audi-
ences were used to, so those presenting Scripture would have done so
from memory.

Speakers would also memorize their presentations because of the
unwieldy nature of ancient scrolls, which, because they were quite

cumbersome, were extremely difficult to read. In a typical scroll the words were compressed tightly to maximize parchment space. There was no punctuation or capitalization, so it was difficult to distinguish words and sentences. Imagine having to decipher the following text:

yetatimeiscomingandhasnowcomewhenthetrueworshiperswill
worshipthefatherinthespiritandintruthfortheyarethekindofwor
shipersthefatherseeksgodisspiritandhisworshipersmustworship
inthespiritandintruth

With concerted effort, a Bible student today would eventually be able to recognize this familiar passage as John 4:23-24. However, imagine having to work through a handwritten manuscript to decode words you have never heard or read before. Such was the daunting task facing Scripture readers in antiquity. Those who presented God's Word would have to know the contents of the text extremely well to read it in public. They might have held the scroll closed in one hand as a symbol of authority, but it was most likely not consulted during a "performance." Scripture readings, therefore, were delivered with a great deal of preparation beforehand, with special attention given to how the text should be communicated.

Uniquely transforming. It might be tempting for us to dismiss as anachronistic our spiritual ancestors' heightened anticipation whenever someone stood up to read Scripture. After all, common people in ancient times did not own Bibles; their only exposure to the sacred writings of the faith occurred via the audio scrolls they heard at church. However, writing off their experience as mere necessity causes us to miss what first-generation Christians found to be true—that reading God's Word aloud in the company of others can be uniquely formative.

When Paul describes the Word of God as profitable for teaching, rebuking, and correcting believers (2 Timothy 3:16-17), the apostle was not picturing Christians having devotions in the privacy of their own homes. Paul envisioned all this rigorous spiritual training happening Sunday morning at church because that's where the people of his day encountered Scripture.

The author of Hebrews, like Paul, was also thinking in terms of Sunday services when he proclaimed that the Word of God is living and active (Hebrews 4:12). Having someone verbalize the text reminded early worshipers that they were hearing God's *living* Word, born by the breath of his Holy Spirit. They conceived God's Word as being *active*, meaning that something happens when God speaks. At creation, every time God spoke his words produced new life (Genesis 1:3, 9). In the same way, God speaking through Scripture activates new life in us. New Testament writers' depicted an encounter with Scripture as a dynamic— living and active—experience, which is why the early Christians considered the public reading of God's Word to be essential for maturation in the faith. N. T. Wright affirms that from the earliest days of Christianity the practice of "soaking oneself in Scripture," both as an individual and as a community, has played a central role in the formation of Christian character.

RECOVERING THE ANCIENT PRACTICE
OF PUBLIC SCRIPTURE READING

An increasing number of churches these days are discovering the unique benefits of reading Scripture aloud together during gathered worship. Many have utilized an ancient spiritual practice known as *lectio divina* (Latin for "divine reading") to orient their congregations toward a more intentionally formative approach to God's Word.

The practice of lectio divina has been handed down to us from the earliest days of the church and is rooted in Judaism. The Jews have always approached the Torah from two distinct perspectives: first, analytically, with the intent of uncovering a single, objective meaning of the text; second, subjectively, in order to arrive at the deeper, more spiritual, more personalized meaning of the passage. Third-century scholar Origen utilized the term *thea anagnosis*, Greek for divine reading, to explain an approach to Scripture that results in receiving a personal message from God. In the sixth century Saint Benedict established lectio divina as one of Western monasticism's foundational spiritual disciplines. Christians have been practicing lectio divina since the early days of the church. Though lectio can be carried out privately or in a group setting, our focus will be using this spiritual discipline in the context of gathered worship.

Corporate lectio divina. Scripture assures us that when the Word of God goes out, it emanates from God himself and does not return to him void; it has a purpose, God does not speak idle words (Isaiah 55:11; Deuteronomy 32:47). Lectio reflects the conviction that God's Word can speak to us in the present moment; it assumes that when God's Word is read, God himself, not a human being, is talking, and the Lord has something important to say to us. As Scripture is read, worshipers are invited to listen for something (a word or phrase) that the Lord might be saying to them and to receive that word as God's personal gift to them. Lectio fosters the expectation, according to Christopher Hall, "that there is a word in the text—an inspired word spoken by the eternal Word made flesh—that is to be believed, obeyed, hugged, devoured, as if all one's life depended on it." Lectio in the context of gathered worship is a here-and-now experience of God's Word that generates a heightened sense of purpose to the reading of Scripture, the exciting possibility that God might speak a significant and relevant word to those who are present.

In a lectio approach Scripture is read without commentary or explanation. While appropriate and necessary in a sermon, exegesis could hinder lectio by directing the listeners' attention to one specific interpretation or application. In lectio the Bible is treated not as a text to be dissected and analyzed but as the living Word of God that, no matter how often we've heard it, is always alive, active, fresh, and new. Lectio assumes that the Word of God is capable of standing on its own. Instead of fulfilling a utilitarian function such as setting up the sermon, Scripture is read for its own sake.

A new way of listening. The writer of Ecclesiastes instructs worshipers to enter the house of God ready to listen instead of being focused on fulfilling some religious obligation (Ecclesiastes 5:1). Reflecting the oral-aural culture of his day, Origen urged his congregation members to listen carefully when Scripture is read because it manifests God's power. Lectio divina demands that we listen for the divine voice behind the human voice whenever Scripture is read aloud in church. Jesus characterizes his sheep—people belonging to his fold—as those who listen for and are able to hear his voice (John 10:27). Lectio, then, is not so much a way of reading as it is a way of listening with an openness to the Spirit's leading.

This ancient spiritual practice invites those of us who have been conditioned by a print culture to experience the Word of God in a new and fresh way—by listening to it instead of reading it. For that reason lectio involves a listening skill that modern Christians may have to learn. It may be awkward at first but hang in there. Like any new skill it takes time to feel comfortable with it. Be patient, especially at the beginning, and don't put undue pressure on yourself to hear a word from God. Avoid working strenuously to find something or make something out of the text; instead, wait patiently for whatever God has for you in it. Lectio favors a patient listening in which we receive the passage and allow it to address us directly; it bids us to allow meaning to unfold and not force it.

Becoming doers of the Word. The main goal of lectio is the ever-deepening transformation of God's people into the image of Christ. In lectio we read and listen to be changed, transformed, recreated, and reshaped into the image of the Word incarnate, Jesus Christ. Mulholland distinguishes famously between reading the Bible for information and reading it for transformation. While I would never devalue the intellectual study of God's Word, a purely academic approach to Scripture results in a lot of head knowledge with little or no experiential understanding. Instead of enabling us to master the text, lectio invites us to approach Scripture in humility with an openness to hear, receive, respond, and be a servant of the Word rather than a master of it. During lectio, we yield to the text, enabling it to become a place of transforming encounter with the Lord.

The epistle to the Hebrews commends the Word of God for its innate ability to cut through our defenses and expose our innermost thoughts and motives (Hebrews 4:12). Wherever God's Word is allowed to penetrate deeply into our being, the Holy Spirit can accomplish God's deepest, most significant work in our lives. When we are reluctant to face the truth about ourselves, lectio forces us to face it; wherever sin has distorted our thinking or our imagination, lectio replaces old thought patterns with new ones. It allows God's Word to renew our minds and reshape the way we think (Romans 12:2).

Another reason lectio is uniquely formative, especially in a group, is because it trains us to respond to the promptings of the Holy Spirit in our lives. As the outline in the next section discloses, corporate lectio encourages participants to share with one another their sense of what the Lord is saying to them as well as any invitation from God to act on what they've heard. Instead of being unaffected by the Word of God, lectio conditions us to be doers of the Word (James 1:22).

BASIC STRUCTURE OF CORPORATE LECTIO DIVINA

Classic lectio divina in a group or congregational setting follows five movements: *silencio, lectio, meditatio, contemplatio,* and *oratio.* For our purposes I will forgo the Latin nomenclature and use their English equivalents. For large groups or congregations I start by inviting

*Wherever
God's Word
is allowed to
penetrate deeply
into our being,
the Holy Spirit
can accomplish
God's deepest,
most significant
work in our lives.*

everyone to form groups of three to four, with the people sitting near them. In a church setting I encourage the congregation to be inclusive and not to leave anyone out. But I also assure visitors and introverts that if they're more comfortable doing the exercise by themselves, that's perfectly fine. I also let everyone know that they don't have to memorize the five steps; I'll guide them through the exercise. All they have to do is enter into the experience, listen, and respond. The following description is written from the perspective of the leader and is drawn from my experience of leading the exercise in large group settings.

Time of quieting. I like to begin with a brief moment of silence to allow people to get settled, quiet their minds, and open their hearts to receive a Word from God.

Time of listening. I then advise the congregation to listen for a word or a phrase in the text that catches their attention—one they're drawn to or that seems to be calling out to them. Then I read the passage slowly. After a brief silence I read the text again in the same manner and invite everyone to share with their group the word or phrase that seems to be speaking to them or that is tugging at their hearts. I tell them not to analyze why they're drawn to that particular word or phrase and not to elaborate when they share it with the group. Merely say the word or phrase that seems to be calling out to them and nothing more at this time. I also ask everyone to go back into silence after sharing. That way, when the room or sanctuary goes totally quiet, I'll know I can proceed.

Time to meditate. When the room quiets, I ask the community to think about how this word touches or relates to their lives as I read the passage again. In other words, what might the Lord be saying to you through this passage? I also let them know that after the reading and a brief silence, I'll invite them to share their thoughts with their group. Then I read the passage again, after which I typically ask, "How is your life touched by this word?" Then I'll signal them to begin sharing their thoughts, cautioning everyone to make it brief, two to four sentences. The rest of the group should listen without interrupting or commenting. I also suggest they begin sharing by saying something like, "I sense the Lord saying to me _____." Again, I remind the group to go back into silence after sharing, so I can discern when to move on.

Time to contemplate. Next, I explain that I'll read the passage one last time followed by a brief silence during which everyone can discern whether there is an invitation for them to act on this word or phrase. In other words, is the Lord calling them to do something as a result of having heard this word or phrase? I then read the passage and ask, "Is there an invitation here for you from the Lord? After a pause I direct the community to share briefly, again preferably two to four sentences, any invitation they're sensing from the reading. If it helps, they could start by saying, "I believe the Lord wants me to _____." Again, group members should listen without interrupting or commenting.

Time to pray. Last, I encourage group members to pray for one another. While this could be conducted in several ways, I typically have them pray for the person on their right, asking the Lord to give that individual the grace and power to respond to the invitation they received from the Lord.

COULD LECTIO BE DANGEROUS?

One question I often hear when I suggest using lectio in church is whether doing so is risky. What if someone "hears" something that is not genuinely from the Spirit? What if they hear what they want to hear and miss what God is really saying? What if someone concludes that God is telling them to do something unscriptural or unlawful, like stealing or killing? Those are all fair questions, and I concede that there's always a risk that people will misinterpret Scripture. However, the same danger lurks to a greater degree for those practicing private devotions. One time a man in my ministry became convinced that God was telling him to leave his wife and kids for a younger woman because God wanted him to be happy. He came to that conclusion after reading his Bible and praying during his daily quiet time. While there is no foolproof way to prevent a person from misappropriating Scripture, corporate lectio potentially safeguards against this possibility by having participants verbalize their impressions of the text to one another. Theoretically, if someone went off the deep end claiming God told them to do something that was blatantly wrong or unlawful, someone in the group would pull that individual aside afterward and lovingly confront them. To clarify, I'm not referring to minor differences in interpretation or doctrine but in those rare occasions when someone deviates from God's Word in a way that could be potentially destructive. A dangerously deceived individual stands a greater chance of being confronted and corrected in small group settings like corporate lectio than if left to themselves.

Preached Versus Unpreached Word

My years of ministry with the Transforming Center have taught me the value of lectio divina and made me appreciate the distinction between the preached and the unpreached Word of God. During our retreats we gather to pray and worship four times a day, and each chapel service features one Scripture reading without comment followed by a moment of silence. At the Transforming Center lectio divina is taught as a spiritual practice—a means of engaging Scripture for the purpose of transformation. As a result of practicing lectio divina each cohort becomes what I consider a "lectio community," meaning that we listen to Scripture readings with a lectio mindset—open and eager to receive a word from

God. We don't need someone to lead us through the five steps every time Scripture is read, because we are accustomed to approaching the Bible as God's Word for us as a community as well as individuals.

As valuable as lectio is, one need not be schooled in this ancient but still popular spiritual discipline to engage meaningfully with the Bible during worship. We can all develop "lectio ears" by understanding the difference between listening to the preached Word and hearing the unpreached Word of God. As mentioned in chapter four, the ancient church developed a three-year cycle of Scripture readings known as the lectionary, which called for four Bible readings at every service in addition to the sermon or homily. Early church practice mirrors the fact that listening to these Bible readings was intended to be a different experience than listening to the sermon. Liturgical churches today still feature Scripture readings without comment. The reading of God's Word does not fulfill a utilitarian function (e.g., setting up the sermon) but constitutes an encounter with God in its own right.

While Scripture reading and sermon are both potentially formative, they're two uniquely different experiences, requiring different listening skills. Sermons tend to be more pedagogical by nature. Congregation members take notes or write down key points because they want to learn something. We may ask, "Lord, what are you trying to teach me through this sermon?" Generally speaking, we listen to sermons to learn something; we listen with our brains.

Hearing the Word of God read apart from the sermon, however, is a less didactic, more subjective experience in which we receive God's spoken Word as coming straight from the mouth of God and addressing us on two levels—both collectively and individually. Thus, we may ask, "Lord, what do you have for me in this passage?" Or "Lord, what are you saying to us in these words?" In Psalm 25, David prays, "Show me your ways, LORD, teach me your paths. Guide me in your truth" (vv. 4-5). Note David's emphasis is on listening to God rather than learning about

God. We listen to the unpreached Word of God more with our hearts than our brains.

This is not to say that one can't learn something from the Scripture reading or to deny that the Lord speaks to us through the sermon. I am suggesting, however, that the two experiences are designed to be different; one speaks to the head, the other to the heart. Together, the preached and the unpreached Word of God offer a holistic approach to Scripture. Put simply, we go to church to hear God speak to us through someone reading his Word *and* someone teaching his Word. Together the public reading of Scripture and the sermon offer powerful ways in which God can communicate to us through his Word.

PRESENTING SCRIPTURE THROUGHOUT THE SERVICE, NOT JUST THE SERMON

I've heard some pastors exhort their congregations not to depend on the church for spiritual nourishment but to learn to feed themselves from God's Word. Their intentions are good; daily devotions are a great idea, but our insistence has created two problems. One is that it's not realistic to expect everyone to have devotions every day. Many try but have trouble being consistent. They're busy working, going to school, or raising families. Another problem is that we've made daily devotions the litmus test for spiritual maturity instead of godly character or the fruits of the Spirit. So when people miss a quiet time here and there, they feel guilty, which makes them reluctant to open their Bibles and pray. Some people give up on regular devotions because they feel like they're not getting anything out of it. They run across Bible passages that they don't understand or seem dry, so they lose interest. Having daily devotions is a wonderful aspiration, but it's not a reasonable expectation to lay on everyone. I believe that those of us who plan and lead worship every Sunday should not operate under the assumption that everyone in the congregation has had their quiet times the whole week. Instead, we should assume they haven't and proceed to bless them with heavy doses of Scripture in our prayers, readings, songs, and sermons. We should look for opportunities to present Scripture throughout the service, not just during the sermon.

Read Scripture like you love it. Scripture readings lend variety to a worship set or a service that could otherwise be dominated by music. Reading a biblical passage to begin the service, transition between songs, or introduce a specific element also helps the congregation to focus on the Lord and lends authority to a worship leader's talking points. Peter reminds church leaders that whenever we speak during worship, we are speaking the very words of God (1 Peter 4:11). When reading Scripture in public, do the Word of God justice and present it with the excellence it deserves. In other words, read Scripture like you love it. Know the passage well; be very familiar with it. Better yet, memorize it if possible. Practice reading aloud; don't let Sunday morning when you're on the platform be the first time you read the passage out loud. Locate any words or phrases that you want to emphasize and experiment beforehand with any vocal inflections or physical gestures you're considering using. God's Word deserves to be read well.

Congregational readings and dramatic presentations. Like prayer, Scripture readings don't have to be a solo act. The congregation can participate. Put the text on a screen or in the bulletin and have worshipers join in a responsive Scripture reading. (See appendix 1 for an example of a typical responsive reading of Scripture.) Some churches periodically invite members to come to the front and share Bible verses along a specific theme. Congregational Scripture readings enable the people to speak the Word of God to one another as well as to themselves. The Bible also lends itself well to dramatic presentations, and not just at Christmas and Easter. Simple and informal presentations without elaborate staging or costumes, known as "readers' theater," can be quite effective. (See appendix 2 for an example of a readers' theater presentation of Scripture.)

Videos depicting biblical scenes and characters or simply scrolling biblical texts are other viable options. The public reading of Scripture can unify the congregation and minister effectively to each member.

Cultivate a lectio community. Many churches today are using lectio divina in their spiritual-formation training. I know pastors who have also taught it from the pulpit. As I experienced in my tenure with the Transforming Center, people who have been introduced to lectio tend to automatically listen to the public reading of Scripture with an openness to receive a word from the Lord. However, as I also stated earlier, gathered worshipers don't need to be knowledgeable about lectio to hear Scripture with lectio ears. Even if lectio is never taught at your church, you can cultivate a lectio community by encouraging those you lead to listen to Scripture readings as God's Word to them individually as well as collectively. Before sharing a Bible passage, invite everyone to listen for a word or phrase that calls for their attention and receive it as a personal message from the Lord. Teach your congregation to regard the reading of God's Word as an invitation to encounter the Lord Jesus Christ.

Transforming worship presents the Bible to both believers and unbelievers as the living Word of God, invested with the power to breathe new life into the souls of all who hear it and receive it.

Eugene Peterson challenges the church to set forth the Bible as the text by which Christians live their lives, for this book stands in stark contrast to "the potpourri of religious psychology, self-development, mystical experimentation, and devotional dilettantism that has come to characterize" today's consumeristic approach to spirituality. Transforming worship presents the Bible to both believers and unbelievers as the living Word of God, invested with the power to breathe new life into the souls of all who hear it and receive it.

8

CORPORATE CONFESSION

The Gift of an Unfettered Conscience

❦

R ECENTLY A PROMINENT EVANGELICAL LEADER and pastor
of a megachurch was accused by several women in his ministry of
making inappropriate sexual advances against them. Confronted with
further allegations of power abuse, deceit, and cover-up, the disgraced
leader resigned. An outside investigative team eventually found the
women's charges to be credible, yet the pastor never apologized but continued to vilify his accusers with claims of collusion. Equally egregious
in my mind is the fact that, after making the results of the investigative
team known, the church never, at any time, publicly called their pastor
to repent.

Within a year, another megachurch pastor across town was fired amid
mounting allegations of financial impropriety, dishonesty, cruel out-
bursts of anger, and the misuse of power. He too never apologized, never
made amends, and played the role of victim. Again, the church fired him
for his inappropriate behavior but failed to call him to repentance.

At this point I should add that confession was not a major theme in
either of these two pastors' sermons, and corporate confession was
rarely if ever practiced at their respective churches. It is troubling that so
many churches today sidestep confession at a time when the abuse of

power is such a serious issue in our culture. While I grieve the damage done to the cause of Christ, I regret even more that these churches missed an opportunity for repentance to be the transforming agent it can be, not only for their two pastors but also for their congregations. In this chapter we will explore the spiritual benefits of corporate confession and imagine a biblically and historically informed vision of repentance for gathered worship in the twenty-first century.

CORPORATE CONFESSION IN SCRIPTURE

Despite the apostle James's clear instruction for Christians to confess their sins to one another (James 5:16), most Protestants think of confession as an exclusively private matter between themselves and God. However, confession, as practiced in the Bible, is a communal spiritual practice as much as it is a private one. The majority of confessions in Scripture are found in the Old Testament, and they are public statements, typical of what an Israelite would share during a worship assembly. Even when occurring privately—as when Saul admits his sin to Samuel (1 Samuel 15:24-25) or David to Nathan (2 Samuel 12:13)—confession still involved some kind of public declaration accompanied by sacrifice or symbolic ritual. The book of Psalms contains several penitential prayers (Psalm 6; 38; 51; 102; 130; 143) that have been prayed corporately as well as privately by God's people since antiquity. The Lord's Prayer, which has been a part of Christian worship since its beginning, contains the familiar confessional phrase, "Forgive us our debts as we have forgiven our debtors" (Matthew 6:12; Luke 11:4). The biblical record discloses that confession is not designed to be merely a private affair, that it should have some kind of regular, public expression in corporate worship.

Patrick Miller identifies two basic formulas behind the confessions recorded in the Old Testament. The first form begins with or contains the simple phrase "I (or we) have sinned." There is no pretense in these prayers, no attempt to rationalize or downplay bad behavior, just a clear and honest admission of guilt. The second type of confessional prayer expounds a bit further by stating "I (or we) have sinned against the Lord." Biblical confessions recognize that our wrongdoings not only hurt fellow human beings but also offend God.

Penitential passages in the psalms are typically presented in general terms but realized on a personal level. For example, by praying "We have done wrong and acted wickedly" (Psalm 106:6), God's people are invited to bring to mind recent examples—specific occurrences—when they behaved wrongly and to confess them. Moreover, the plural pronouns that appear in these confessional psalms are significant in that they capture our solidarity with the sinfulness that permeates society. The *we* pronouns spoken in public confession help guard against self-righteousness and judgmentalism by reminding us that, despite our external religiosity (which is on full display every Sunday at church), we too are sinners in need of forgiveness. The biblical models of corporate confession invite us to consider not only our individual sinful actions but also our complicity in the sins that define the human condition, such as "the lust of the flesh, the lust of the eyes, and the pride of life" (1 John 2:16).

Confession, as practiced in the Bible, is a communal spiritual practice as much as it is a private one.

New Testament writers exhibit continuity with their Old Testament counterparts by presenting confession as an act of prayer that is enhanced by some kind of social expression. James 5:15-16, for example, specifically directs Christians to confess their sins to one another and pray for each so that they may be healed of their sicknesses. While some commentators limit the text's application to physical healing, biblical scholar Grant Osborne is among those who broaden its interpretation to include all types of healing—emotional, psychological, spiritual as well as physical. Scripture invites us to consider the healing properties of mutual confession as essential to a congregation's overall spiritual health.

In addition to underscoring the value of corporate confession, the New Testament also heightens the need for repentance. Since all of us have sinned and fallen short of the glory of God (Romans 3:23), Christians have an urgent and continual need to confess their sinfulness to one another before God. In the Judeo-Christian tradition, confession is not just a private matter; there is a public dimension to it that should not be ignored.

Corporate Confession in the Church

The *Didache* exhorted first-century Christ-followers to confess their failings publicly so as not to remain overwhelmed by a guilty conscience. The framers of the *Didache* trusted Christian fellowship to be a safe and supportive environment for sharing one's sins and shortcomings. Interestingly, extant documents do not indicate that the earliest church services included prayers of confession. Hughes Oliphant Old explains the exclusion by clarifying that confession played a major role initially in the church's weekday prayer meetings but eventually found its way into gathered worship, where, by the late sixth century, it became a regular feature in the Sunday liturgy. Miller adds that the early church's understanding of sin as intrinsic to the human condition is one of the reasons mutual confession found its way into gathered worship. Including corporate confession regularly in Sunday services makes an important statement about the reality of sin in our lives.

The Middle Ages witnessed an emphasis on the penitential psalms during worship. During the medieval period, confessors were also required to make personal confession to a priest, name specific sins, and perform penance to atone for their transgressions. The Reformation signaled major changes in the church's approach to corporate confession. Rejecting what they saw as abuses of the Catholic Church, Reformers crafted new prayers intended to reflect a more biblical understanding of sin and repentance. Reformation leaders also removed requirements to confess personally to a priest and insisted on restoring the practice of public confession and absolution established by the ancient church. Today, most liturgically minded traditions—Anglican, Episcopalian, Catholic, Eastern Orthodox, and mainline Protestant churches—include weekly confession during worship, while nondenominational and free churches feature it occasionally or, sadly, not at all. Historically though, corporate confession has played a valuable role in Christian communities since the beginning of our faith.

CONFESSION AS A FORMATIVE SPIRITUAL PRACTICE

Ruth Barton teaches that an increasing awareness of our un-Christlike behavior is an inevitable part of the spiritual journey:

> As we become more spiritually attuned, we become painfully aware of how negative thought patterns and relating patterns hurt ourselves and others. We see the places where we are incapable of love and true self-giving. We realize that our responses to wounds we've received have caused us to become hard and self-protective. We notice the subtleties of our jealousies, our mean-spiritedness, our manipulations, our controlling ways, and our mistrust of God and others that keeps us from giving ourselves wholeheartedly. Having tried every self-help approach we know, we are devastated to admit that real, fundamental change is beyond our reach. The heart cries out to be free from its bondage.

By opening us up to the transforming work of God in our life, the spiritual practice of confession offers the possibility of greater freedom from sin.

A formative approach to confession begins with some healthy and constructive form of self-examination. In many ways, the term *self*-examination is a bit of a misnomer; we're not examining ourselves. We're asking the Holy Spirit to show us the truth about ourselves; we're beseeching the Lord to reveal to us our faults and failures. Barton clarifies that self-examination awakens us to the presence of God as God really is and also makes us aware of ourselves as we really are. In Psalm 139, after acknowledging that God is omniscient and omnipresent and that, as God's child, he is "fearfully and wonderfully made," David invites God to examine his life:

> Search me, God, and know my heart;
>> test me and know my anxious thoughts.
> See if there is any offensive way in me,
>> and lead me in the way everlasting. (vv. 23-24)

Self-examination fosters the kind of humility and openness that allows us to hear the truth about ourselves.

Patrick Miller insists that sin, as portrayed in the Bible, is never an abstract notion but is, instead "a warp in the divine order, a breakdown in the nature of relationship, a moral breach that always has consequences, however small they may be, and damages the way things are meant to be among ourselves and with God." After convicting us of sin, the Holy Spirit does not leave us wallowing in despair but instead instills a desire to confess our iniquities to God in order to straighten out the warp, restore relationship, and repair the breach. Confession requires us to take responsibility not only for the outward manifestations of our sinfulness but also for the underlying causes that produce the wrong behavior in the first place. Confession invites us to say our failures out loud to ourselves, to God, and to those we have hurt, to renounce our wrongdoing, and make restitution where it's required.

David penned Psalm 51 after being confronted about his affair with Bathsheba. Broken and contrite, David takes full responsibility for his sin. "Have mercy on me, O God," he cries. "Blot out my transgressions" (v. 1). He doesn't make excuses or blame anyone else. He is well aware of his terrible deeds, that he has made horrible moral choices (v. 3). He owns up to the fact that he, of his own volition, offended a holy God (v. 4). David asks the Lord to cleanse him and wash away his sin (vv. 2, 7) and to allow him to experience joy instead of shame and remorse (v. 8). At the heart of genuine repentance is a longing to be cleansed, to be set free from the bondage of our sinful habits. At this point confession is becoming formational for David; he wants to be a better, more godly man. "Create in me a pure heart, O God," he cries out, "and renew a steadfast spirit within me" (v. 10). David wants to change, but he knows he can't do that by sheer willpower. He calls out to God to create something new in him, a new heart and a renewed spirit. Self-examination and confession enable us to embrace divine forgiveness, thereby putting us on the path to spiritual renewal and change. God gently leads us to name our sin so we can be healed from the pain and destruction it brings into our lives and into the world. Self-examination and confession, then, go hand-in-hand as effective tools for transformation.

THE UNIQUE ROLE OF CORPORATE CONFESSION IN SPIRITUAL FORMATION

Corporate confession as a formative spiritual practice honors the fact that no one can move forward in the Christian life until we are honest with God and ourselves about our current spiritual condition. You may recall from chapter three the individual who visited the first-century church of Corinth and was convicted of sin during a church service; the secrets of his heart were disclosed and he dropped to his knees (1 Corinthians 14:24-25). In other words he came face-to-face with his inner thoughts and motives and could no longer deny, ignore, or hide the reality that he was a sinful man in need of the Savior. The Holy Spirit was calling him to repent and change his ways. What happened to our Corinthian friend illustrates the power of public confession to transform lives.

Self-examination and confession enable us to embrace divine forgiveness, thereby putting us on the path to spiritual renewal and change.

Despite the importance of examining our lives and confessing our errors, few Christians actually do it; even fewer make a regular practice of it. Yet most of us are aware, at least intuitively, that we are seriously flawed human beings. We see a gap between who we desire to be and who we really are, a discrepancy between how we want to live and how we behave. Paul admitted that he struggled to do the good he wanted to do, that no matter how hard he tried, sin was always there to sabotage his efforts to obey God (Romans 7:14-23). Yet he wanted to have a clear conscience both before God and before fellow human beings (Acts 24:16). Like all of us, Paul didn't want to be at odds with anybody, especially God. The only way to achieve a blameless conscience is to make sure that we don't go for any length of time with unconfessed sin eating away at our souls. Churches that regularly include the opportunity for worshipers to confess sin offer their congregants a valuable gift—an unfettered conscience.

A spiritually healthy approach to repentance in public worship follows a three-part process that begins with self-evaluation, then moves to confession, and ends with an assurance of forgiveness. While some conceive of repentance as strictly a private affair, I have found the three-step progression of self-examination, confession, and absolution, practiced in a corporate setting, to be a uniquely formative experience that cannot be duplicated.

Self-examination with God's love as the starting point. A healthy and formative process of public repentance begins with an honest assessment of ourselves. However, many of us avoid self-examination because it often digresses into a negative exercise in self-loathing. Who wants to be constantly reminded that they don't measure up? Who wants to feel like a failure? Self-examination should never become a degrading, shame-inducing experience. Continual self-flagellation is more deforming than transforming. The key to opening up ourselves to God's scrutiny in a truly edifying way is to first recognize that God is loving, merciful, and good. Barton agrees that self-examination, rightly practiced, leads us into a greater awareness of God's constant, loving presence and thereby offers us a safe place to face the truth about ourselves. A healthy process of self-examination and confession begins with the acknowledgment that God is loving and that we are God's beloved people.

In Psalm 26, David invites the Lord to test him, try him, and examine his heart and mind (v. 2). He knows he can't live a life of integrity without God's help. David feels safe availing himself of God's honest appraisal because he is ever mindful of God's unfailing love (v. 3). David is able to hear constructive criticism without plunging into a paralyzing state of depression because he knows God loves him and has his best interest in mind. If the Lord brings to mind something he needs to repent of or an area of his life that needs attention, David is glad and thankful; instead of feeling threatened, he welcomes God's thorough examination of his life. As the fourth-century theologian Augustine worked through this psalm, he was prompted to pray for his eyes to always be fixed on God's mercy so he would not be overwhelmed or consumed by God's "purging fire." When Paul exhorts us to examine ourselves or test ourselves (2 Corinthians 13:5), he envisions doing so in the presence of the God who welcomes us with open arms into his loving presence (2 Corinthians 6:16-18). Scripture affirms that it is God's kindness that leads us to true repentance (Romans 2:4).

One can certainly encounter God's love during private devotions. However, gathered worship offers a unique opportunity to receive the love of God anew. The psalmist sings, "Within your temple, O God, we meditate on your unfailing love" (Psalm 48:9). Church is to be a place that proclaims God's love, that joyfully celebrates the fact that our God is loving, gracious, and good. Even if we're having trouble believing that God loves us, hearing God's love spoken, sung, or prayed over us at church invites us to claim it for ourselves.

Confession in the context of a loving community. Confessing wrong behavior in community with others assures us that we are not alone in our sin. Dietrich Bonhoeffer teaches that one of the telltale signs of authentic community is the ability to be together not as perfect, devout people but as undevout sinners. By contrast, where there's inauthentic community, no one is permitted to be a sinner, so everyone conceals their sins from one another and continues to live in lies and hypocrisy. Bonhoeffer warns that one who is alone with their sin is utterly alone. Communities that do not practice regular confession communicate the false perception that good Christians do not struggle with sin. So their members deny or hide their darkest thoughts and bad behavior. Being left alone and alienated in our sin encourages more sin.

The truth is, we all struggle with temptation, we all have blind spots, and we all perpetuate dysfunctional ways of being and living. It's painful to admit those things, but deep down inside we know that we are seriously flawed human beings living in a severely broken world. The prophet Isaiah encountered the holiness of God during worship and was instantly confronted with his sinfulness. "Woe to me!" he cried. "I am ruined! For I am a man of unclean lips, and I live among a people of unclean lips" (Isaiah 6:5). Corporate confession, especially in conjunction with worship, invites us to follow Isaiah's example and name what we already sense is true about ourselves—that we are flawed.

Confessing while surrounded by Christian brothers and sisters committed to loving us can prevent those who are perfectionistic from slipping into a downward spiral of self-hatred over their faults and deficiencies. Public confession reminds us that we are still loved by God and by others even when we fail, that God can take even our mistakes and do something redemptive with them. Confession in the context of a loving, grace-filled community can also strengthen our resolve to live for Christ. No one can defeat sin on their own; we need each other's help to live an obedient Christian life. Confessing in the context of worship enables us to draw strength from one another when we are weak.

Finally, communal confession calls us to take responsibility for any part we've played in society's ills. The church's prayer of confession, writes Mark Labberton, "takes us into the darkness of our own hearts and of the world. . . . It dares to proclaim, on a personal and collective level, for those inside and outside the church, that sin and evil are real and destructive." Confessing sin during worship challenges God's people to admit any complicity on our part in the oppression, violence, injustice, and abuse of power that wreak death and destruction throughout our world. Confession in the context of a loving community, therefore, prevents us from living in isolation with our sin, strengthens us in faithful obedience, and summons us to stand in solidarity with all who suffer the heinous effects of sin.

Receiving divine absolution. In traditional Christian worship, corporate repentance culminates with words of absolution, announcing that all who have confessed their sins are indeed forgiven. The absolution assures worshipers, especially those who are weighed down by guilt and burdened by sin and failure, that all is forgiven, that they are free to walk a new path. The absolution is usually based on a Bible verse such as Psalm 103:12: "As far as the east is from the west, so far has [God] removed our transgressions from us." Though typically spoken by a pastor or priest, the absolution, because it is scriptural, is understood to be God speaking to us, ensuring that God, not our sin, has the final word in our repentance.

Another common example of absolution comes from 1 John 1:9: "If we confess our sins, [God] is faithful and just and will forgive us our sins and purify us from all unrighteousness." Notice the eagerness with which God forgives sin. Curt Thompson insightfully observes that John doesn't give us a two-step process in which we confess our sin and then ask for God's forgiveness; there is no intermediary step. It's as if divine forgiveness fills the room, "waiting for us, and confession merely opens our hearts to receive its flood of relief, joy, and freedom." God is quick to forgive because he doesn't want us to remain in the shame of our sin but wants to meet us in it so he can rewrite our stories. God knows how much damage wallowing in guilt and shame can do to the human psyche. Our merciful God realizes how important it is for human beings to feel accepted and know they are loved, so as soon as we confess our sin, he immediately assures us that we are forgiven.

In Psalm 32, David expresses the joy of being forgiven. He begins by proclaiming how much of a blessing it is to have our transgressions blotted out, covered, and no longer counted against us (vv. 1-2). David then shares from his personal experience, admitting that when he kept quiet about his sin, he was tortured by guilt and shame (vv. 3-4). The moment David acknowledged and confessed his wrong-doing, God forgave him (v. 5). The psalm ends with David, free from guilt and shame, rejoicing in the Lord and singing God's praises (v. 11). Though God's compassionate love was always there, David couldn't receive it because unconfessed sin had placed a barrier between him and God; he knew he wasn't right with the Lord. As soon as David confessed, God extended a full pardon. At that point David embraced forgiveness and celebrated that he was once again right with the Lord.

A Formative Approach to Corporate Confession in Your Setting

Given its far-reaching benefits, churches desiring a spiritually formative approach to worship should, first, consider making confession a regular (preferably weekly) practice in their Sunday services if it isn't already. I encourage all churches to offer their congregations the full progression beginning with self-evaluation, moving to confession, and ending with absolution. Church practice varies about where to position confession in the service. Lutherans, for example, practice confession toward the beginning of the worship order. They reason that one does not come to worship or enter into God's presence harboring unconfessed sin. Other liturgical traditions practice confession before Communion. For churches without a set liturgy or tradition, it is conceivable to vary the order from week to week, featuring confession at the beginning of the music set, before Communion, or after the sermon, whichever seems most appropriate for that week's service. In all cases I also suggest adding appropriate amounts of creativity and variety to prevent the experience from becoming rote or perfunctory. Give careful consideration to your demeanor as you lead your people through confession. Be sure to set a warm, pastoral tone and exude genuine love and care for your people as you guide them through a formative experience of repentance.

Self-evaluation with God for the people of God. In many churches the first movement—self-evaluation—is accomplished through a moment of silence, which can be introduced verbally or in print as a time for personal reflection, prayer, listening, preparation, or merely being present to God. Ranging anywhere from twenty to sixty seconds, this brief pause in the service is sometimes supported with soft music playing in the background or an image projected on the screen—a tranquil nature scene, for example. The words to Psalm 139:23-24 could also be sung, prayed, or projected:

> Search me, God, and know my heart;
> > test me and know my anxious thoughts.
> See if there is any offensive way in me,
> > and lead me in the way everlasting.

Other Scriptures commonly used to set up the reflection time are Matthew 22:37-40 ("Love the Lord your God with all your heart . . . and your neighbor as yourself"), 1 John 1:8-9 ("If we claim to be without sin, we deceive ourselves"), and Hebrews 4:14, 16 ("approach God's throne of grace with confidence"). A short pastoral prayer is sometimes inserted to bring the reflection time to a close and to set up the confession that follows.

Liturgical churches tend to be amenable to the idea of incorporating silence in worship. I realize, however, that for many churches this could be a new and foreign concept. Nevertheless, offering people a quiet respite from the noise and busyness of their lives is a gift they rarely receive anywhere else. The practice of silence in corporate worship can be a breath of fresh air in our increasingly frenetic, high-stress world. If silence is new to your church, I suggest introducing it in a way that helps your people engage quickly and easily. Explain the benefits of quiet reflection and why we do it; offer practical ideas on what to do or what to think about during the silence; start with twenty seconds and lengthen it as time goes on. The experience may feel awkward for some people at first, but be patient and keep encouraging worshipers to be present to God as best they can during the silence. The psalmist exhorts all those gathered for worship to be still and know that the one we worship is God (Ps 46:10). I can't think of a better place to experience some much-needed peace and quiet than in church.

I am aware that some confession liturgies do not include a time of self-examination. They observe a brief moment of silence during which worshipers are invited to confess their sins privately to the Lord. Doing that occasionally is fine but not regularly because it shortchanges the self-evaluation process. Remember that the goal here is a formative approach to confession that helps a congregation realize its psychological and spiritual benefits. To ensure that people are led to repentance by God's lovingkindness instead of self-hatred (Romans 2:4), the confessional part of the service should begin with some affirmation—whether spoken or sung—of God's love. A song emphasizing God's love, grace, goodness, or mercy, for example, enables worshipers to internalize the love of God. Psalm 139:13-14 could also be shared to underscore that God knows us and loves us:

> You created my inmost being;
>> you knit me together in my mother's womb.
> I praise you because I am fearfully and wonderfully made;
>> your works are wonderful,
>> I know that full well.

I visited a Lutheran church recently and was treated to the following pastoral prayer, which did an excellent job of setting our confession time within the framework of God's gracious love:

> PASTOR. God begins the process of making us new by convicting our hearts of sin so his message of amazing forgiveness and love is ready to be received. He calls us to confess those sins before him and receive his gift of forgiveness won for us on the cross and assured by his resurrection from the grave. No matter where you are in your walk with God, his grace is here for you right now. His forgiving love is here to wash away your sin. In the quiet of these moments, pour out your heart to him and let him have you—all of you. (*Quiet moments for personal prayer and confession.*)

Helping your people stay mindful of God's love as they reflect on their sins ensures that the repentance process gets off on the right foot.

Confession before God with the people of God. In line with the biblical models, confessions for gathered worship typically use *we* and *us* pronouns. Prayers are worded in a way that is specific, not vague or ambiguous, while still allowing for a wide range of applications, which guarantees that everyone can pray them authentically.

If corporate confession is not a common practice in your church and you'd like to introduce it, you could have a leader say something like,

"Let us confess our sins in the presence of God and of one another." Regarding what words to use for the actual confession, most hymnals and several prayer books offer a wide variety of choices. My favorite combines verbiage from both the Lutheran and Episcopalian churches and starts with the leader addressing God and the people joining in.

LEADER. Most merciful God.

RESPONSE. We confess that we have sinned against you in thought, word, and deed, by what we have done and by what we have left undone. We have not loved you with our whole heart; we have not loved our neighbors as ourselves. We are truly sorry and we humbly repent. For the sake of your Son Jesus Christ, have mercy on us. Please forgive us, renew us, and lead us, so that we may delight in your will and walk in your ways, to the glory of your holy name. Amen.

The Book of Common Worship also includes several prayers for confession, my favorite is a bit lengthy, but it's nicely arranged as a responsive reading so the congregation can actively participate (see appendix 3).

I encourage leaders who already use set prayers for confession to break out of the routine occasionally and bring a fresh insight or encouraging word so people don't go on autopilot during confession. For example, encourage worshipers to think of a specific time during the past week when they didn't show love to someone and to express their regret to the Lord silently before corporate confession. Invite those who came to church feeling guilty or ashamed about something they said or did this week to confess their remorse silently to our gracious, merciful God. We all deal with discouragement to some degree over our moral failures and weaknesses. Inviting your people to offer confession in the company of loving Christian friends reminds them that they are not alone in their sin.

Blessed assurance. In addition to Psalm 103:12 and 1 John 1:9, the liturgical tradition presents a wide variety of options for absolution.

The New Handbook of the Christian Year contains a delightful exchange between pastor and congregation that upholds gathered worship as a dynamic expression of the priesthood of believers. After public confession the minister says to the people, "Hear the good news: Christ died for us while we were yet sinners; that proves God's love toward us. In the name of Jesus Christ, you are forgiven!" The people then address their pastor with assuring words of pardon: "In the name of Jesus Christ, you are forgiven!" Then all exclaim, "Glory to God. Amen."

Some denominations prefer that the words of pardon come from an ecclesiastical authority figure. After confession in many Lutheran churches, a minister declares, "In the mercy of almighty God, Jesus Christ was given to die for us, and for his sake God forgives us all our sins. As a called and ordained minister of the church of Christ, and by his authority, I therefore declare to you the entire forgiveness of all your sins, in the name of the Father, and of the Son, and of the Holy Spirit. Amen." Please don't underestimate the power of absolution in worship. Offering your congregation assurance of forgiveness is one of the most renewing and restorative moments of the entire service.

Martin Luther began his ninety-five theses by stating that all believers are to live a life of repentance. The three-step approach to confession outlined earlier effectively teaches God's people how to live lives of repentance. Practicing self-examination with God's love as the starting point, making confession in the context of a loving community, and receiving divine absolution combine to make repentance in worship a healing and restorative grace of God that sets us free from the burden of guilt and shame.

Offering your congregation assurance of forgiveness is one of the most renewing and restorative moments of the entire service.

9

LORD'S SUPPER AS
SPIRITUAL NOURISHMENT

✥

SEVERAL YEARS AGO I met Sister Pam, a retired nun. We were
classmates in an extensive training program for spiritual directors.
Though we came from diverse backgrounds, Sister Pam and I quickly
became friends and shared numerous conversations about spiritual life.
What impressed me most about my Catholic sister was her deep love
and genuine passion for the Lord's Supper. When Sister Pam spoke of
the Eucharist, as she called it, her eyes lit up with delight and there was
an exhilarating enthusiasm in her voice. Despite communing daily, the
sacrament is not an obligatory ritual for her but an opportunity to encounter Jesus in a deeply profound way.

My experience of Communion pales in comparison to that of my
newfound friend. Though my Protestant upbringing has served me well,
the teaching I received on the Lord's Supper over the years was dominated by a vehement rejection of transubstantiation, staunch insistence
that the bread and wine are mere symbols, and the avoidance of any
reference to a real presence of Christ. My tradition downplayed any real
presence of Jesus to such a degree that I struggled to experience Christ
at all during this sacred act. Communion was always presented as a time
to remember how sinful I am and that Jesus died for my sins, so it was a

highly cerebral exercise. It was always sad and somber, like a memorial or funeral. What I have discovered in recent years is that my experience is not uncommon. I have heard other Protestants echo similar frustrations—that the Lord's Supper reminds them that Jesus died for their sins but rarely fosters an encounter with the living Christ. Unfortunately, this limited view of Communion hinders worshipers from experiencing its full benefits.

VITAL SPIRITUAL NOURISHMENT

From the earliest days of the church, the Eucharist has been regarded as spiritual nourishment. According to Justin Martyr the first generation of Christians understood that the bread and wine were intended to nourish their entire being for transformation. The pioneers of our faith regarded bread and wine as spiritual food. For them, Communion was part of fulfilling their baptismal commitment to grow in Christlikeness. From the beginning the edification of believers has been and always will be the purpose of the sacred meal.

Later Christian writers were even more effusive in articulating a high view of Communion. Penned in the early fifteenth century, Thomas à Kempis's classic work, *The Imitation of Christ*, describes the Eucharist as

> the salvation of our soul and body and the medicine for every spiritual illness. In this sacrament we have a cure for our wickedness and a curb to our passions. In addition, it conquers or reduces temptation, pours greater grace into our hearts, gives growth to virtue, fortifies our faith, strengthens our hope, and enkindles and expands our love.

John Calvin's vision of the Lord's Supper echoes the high premium his predecessors' put on the sacrament for spiritual sustenance:

> When the bread is given as a symbol of Christ's body, we must at once grasp this comparison: as bread nourishes, sustains, and

keeps life in our body, so Christ's body is the only food to invig-
orate and enliven our soul. When we see wine set forth as a symbol
of blood, we must reflect on the benefits which wine imparts to
the body, and so realize that the same are spiritually imparted to
us by Christ's blood. These benefits are to nourish, refresh,
strengthen, and gladden.

For followers of Jesus Christ, Communion is more than merely an occasion for remembering personal sinfulness; it is vital nutrition for the
soul, a lifeline in a Christian's journey toward spiritual wholeness. To understand why patristic and Reformation writers recognized the Eucharist
as a formative experience, one must understand what they meant when
they spoke of partaking of the elements in remembrance of Christ.

In remembrance of Christ. For the ancients, Jesus' command to
partake of the elements in remembrance of him (Luke 22:19; 1 Corinthians 11:24-25) was more than merely an exercise in memory recall.
The phrase *in remembrance* is translated from the more
finely nuanced Greek word *anamnēsis* and implies
that we live in the present enlightened by our

> *Communion
> is more than
> merely an occasion
> for remembering
> personal sinfulness;
> it is vital nutrition
> for the soul,
> a lifeline in a
> Christian's journey
> toward spiritual
> wholeness.*

memories of past events, that we allow the
past to shape, inform, and penetrate the
present. To eat the bread and drink the cup in
remembrance of Christ is to recall the death
and resurrection of our Savior with such vivid-
ness as to make ourselves present to these
events not merely as historical occurrences
but as present, living, and transforming
realities in our lives today.

In the remainder of this chapter, I will frame
these spiritually formative qualities of the Lord's
Supper around three theological truths: the Table
(1) unites God's people to the transforming

presence of Christ, (2) unites believers to form communities in which spiritual transformation occurs, and (3) enlists grateful worshipers to continue Christ's transforming work of redemption and renewal in the world.

UNITED TO THE TRANSFORMING PRESENCE OF CHRIST

Recalling our discussion of the Emmaus story from chapter two, the two Emmaus disciples finally recognized who Jesus was when he took bread, gave thanks, broke it, and handed it to them (Luke 24:28-31). As Jesus broke the bread, the two Emmaus pilgrims finally realized they were in the presence of Christ. Emmaus illustrates how Jesus' disciples can experience his presence after the resurrection—that is, in breaking bread together. Brant Pitre suggests that Cleopas and his comrade were kept from recognizing Jesus initially because, henceforth, he would be uniquely known to them—through breaking bread together:

> Jesus was pointing them to the way he would be present with them from now on. After his ascension into heaven, he would no longer be with them under the appearance of a man. . . . He would only be present under the appearance of the eucharistic bread. . . . And in his risen body, he is no longer bound by space, or time, or even appearance. The risen Jesus can appear when he wills, where he wills, how he wills, and under whatever form he wills.

For we who have not experienced the earthly Jesus, the Emmaus story offers the Eucharist as a concrete, effective means of entering into the presence of the risen Christ.

Any discussion about the presence of Christ at the Communion Table can potentially stir controversy. The dispute surrounding how Jesus is present in the bread and wine has divided Catholics and Protestants for centuries. Modern Christians may be surprised to learn that the early church felt no pressure to explain how the bread and wine became Jesus' flesh and blood. Justin Martyr states matter-of-factly that in the same way that Christ was made flesh by a word of God, so the elements consecrated by a word of prayer become "the flesh and blood of that incarnate Christ." The New Testament church was not concerned about a specific moment when the bread and wine materialized into the body and blood of Jesus, yet the reality of Christ's eucharistic presence was strongly proclaimed and therefore assumed from the beginning of the Christian faith. For the fledgling church, how the bread and wine became the body of Christ was beside the point; Communion offered a genuine encounter with Jesus for spiritual strengthening.

All attempts to explain how the bread and wine become the living Christ are secondary, therefore, to the gift of Christ's presence that is received at the Table. John Calvin asserts that Christians should participate in the Lord's Supper as if Christ himself is present: "set before our eyes and touched by our hands." The bread and wine do not constitute the only form Christ's presence can take, but the Eucharist is certainly one of the most unique manifestations of Jesus' presence. Both Protestants and Catholics should be careful that we not become so preoccupied with explaining how Jesus is present in the elements that we miss the deeper reality that he is truly with us as we gather around the Communion Table. Jesus himself said that his flesh is "real food" and his blood is "real drink" (John 6:55). Jesus is really present at the Table. The Lord's Supper unites God's people to the transforming presence of Christ, wherein, through the power of the Holy Spirit, we encounter Jesus, receive forgiveness, and are invited to reaffirm our desire to live for him.

Encountering Jesus. Christians are invited to come to the Table not merely to reminisce or think about Jesus but to encounter Jesus, to take Christ fully into ourselves to such an extent that he becomes part of us. We are to approach Communion anticipating "a divine encounter," as Leech puts it, "to consume and be consumed." In the bread and cup Jesus himself invites us to abide in ever-deepening communion with him

(John 6:56). The Lord's Supper draws us into intimate fellowship with the risen Christ.

Communing with the risen Christ means that we encounter both the humanity and divinity of Jesus. Everything Jesus offered his first disciples—for example, healing, reconciliation, salvation, wisdom—is available to us when we encounter Christ at his table. Encountering Jesus during Communion also makes available everything that the divine Son of God offers as our heavenly high priest (Hebrews 4:14), advocate (1 John 2:1-2), and intercessor (Hebrews 7:25). To encounter Christ during the Lord's Supper, then, is to avail ourselves of every spiritual blessing needed for spiritual formation (Ephesians 1:3). The Table unites us to Christ, wherein we encounter the transforming presence of our Savior.

Experiencing forgiveness. The Eucharist is not merely a cognitive exercise that reminds us that our sins are forgiven but also an opportunity to experience God's forgiveness in a fresh and meaningful way. In the same way that Jesus demonstrated love and acceptance to sinners by eating with them, Jesus extends the same kind of love to all who gather around the bread and wine, accepting them as friends. Because the Lord's Supper is a communal experience, it puts us in touch with our fellow human beings. Hence, the forgiveness we experience alongside God's people at the Communion Table reminds us and empowers us to forgive others. The Lord's Supper, therefore, enables believers to encounter Christ and receive pardon for our sins and to be transformed into people who extend grace, mercy, and forgiveness to others.

Reaffirming our desire to live for Christ. The Table also offers worshipers an opportunity to renew our covenant relationship with God through Jesus Christ. Since Jesus stipulated that the Communion cup represents the new covenant in his blood (Luke 22:20; 1 Corinthians 11:25), Christians have commonly viewed the Lord's Supper as a covenantal meal—an opportunity for Jesus' followers to renew or reaffirm their commitment to follow Christ. The Table, according to Leech, reminds disciples that a commitment to Christ entails living a life of sacrifice: "In this sense, the eucharistic sacrifice is a microcosm of the whole Christian life, which is dying and rising with Christ, a process of life through death, a metamorphosis." When we partake of the bread and the wine, we are committing ourselves to live a certain way—God's way. Communion invites God's people to be shaped and molded by a sincere desire to live a committed, loyal, and sacrificial Christian life.

UNITED TO ONE ANOTHER IN
TRANSFORMING COMMUNITIES

In Paul's first letter to the Corinthians he charges them with abusing the Lord's Supper. To correct their behavior he offers instruction in chapters 10 and 11 that highlights the sacrament's spiritually formative potential to build and strengthen community. Paul begins his discourse with the extraordinary claim that the Communion elements establish church unity. By gratefully receiving the cup (1 Corinthians 10:16), for example, believers participate in the blood of Christ and share in the benefits of his death and resurrection. The word translated "participation," the Greek word *koinonia,* means communal participation or sharing. Instead of a group of detached people with their own experiences, the cup draws us together into a shared identity as God's people, whose very lifeblood is the blood of Christ. In the same way the bread brings us together as a family gathered around a meal, coming together to share one loaf of bread (1 Corinthians 10:17). Paul uses the words *come together* several times in 1 Corinthians 11. This phrase, in the original Greek, connotes diverse people joining together in community or adversaries being united. Paul emphasizes togetherness to the Corinthians because their observances of Communion had become divisive (1 Corinthians 11:17-18). When they came together as a church they were anything but together in the truest sense of the word. In Corinth the Lord's Supper had deteriorated into a ritual solely for personal edification instead of the unifying communal reality it was intended to be. We will explore the major cause of the division later, but for now suffice it to say that the church at Corinth was a fractured community.

To correct their divisive attitudes and behavior, Paul calls the Christians at Corinth back to the Upper Room to reconsider the words Jesus spoke at the Last Supper—what we now refer to as the Words of Institution (1 Corinthians 11:23-26). Paul draws on these familiar words and images to remind the Corinthians of the foundational meaning of community and to realign them around their purpose as the body of Christ in the world.

Leonard Vander Zee rightly concludes that "the Lord's Supper not only gathers a community, it creates a community." The bond of friendship enjoyed by those who gather for the Eucharist has its roots in the mealtime practices of our Jewish ancestors; for the ancient Hebrews, eating together created unity among those sharing the meal, not only symbolizing their loyalty to one another but actually establishing it. The first-century Greco-Roman world perpetuated the idea that mealtimes brought people together socially, obligating them to one another in friendship. Gathered in the Upper Room with his disciples, Jesus referred to those who broke bread with him as friends, instructing them to love one another as he had loved them (John 15:12-15). The Christian sacrament of Communion, therefore, emerged amid a culture that valued table fellowship as an expression of unity and friendship.

The Lord's Supper is both a declaration and manifestation of Christian unity not only with those who are physically present in the moment but also with the entire Christian community worldwide. When we eat the bread and drink the cup together, we become that which we receive— the historically vibrant and dynamic body of Christ. The Lord's Supper then creates an eternal community bound together in Jesus Christ and unites us to Christians everywhere—past, present, and future. Our second theological truth focuses on the communal nature of the Eucharist: the Lord's Supper, experienced in the context of authentic community, fosters spiritual formation by holding us accountable to initiate reconciliation and challenging us to overcome our differences.

Learning to initiate reconciliation. Jesus taught that while approaching the altar, if we remember that a brother or sister has something against us, we should leave our gifts at the altar, go and be reconciled to that individual, and then return to offer our gifts (Matthew 5:23-24). Reflecting Jesus' urgency to resolve relational conflict, the *Didache* required churchgoers who were at odds with each other to be reconciled before coming to the Lord's table. Centuries later John Calvin warned his congregants not to approach the Communion Table if they were harboring any hatred, bitterness, or malice against anyone, especially fellow believers in the church. In the Christian tradition worshipers are expected to resolve factions and relational discord, especially with one another, before receiving the bread and the wine.

The forgiveness believers experience at the Communion Table empowers us to take the first step in restoring broken relationships by forgiving those who have wronged us. Because Communion necessitates reconciliation, the Table is where the church becomes a reconciled community amid a broken and fragmented world. Alexander Schmemann adds that in and through the Lord's Supper, God's people are restored to that authentic community and loving solidarity which, sadly, the world has lost. The Eucharist unites God's people to form communities in which we experience spiritual transformation by submitting to the hard work of relational reconciliation that being part of the body of Christ demands.

Overcoming our differences. Learning to resolve conflicts enables God's people to overcome our differences. The disciples were a diverse bunch of guys. They came from all walks of life, different backgrounds, different social circles. They had differing opinions and divergent political views. They fought and argued with each other. Yet friendship with Jesus bound them together as friends and enabled them to overcome their differences. Gathering around a table with Jesus and eating together was an expression of their unity. The same thing happens today when friends of Jesus gather for the Lord's Supper; we become a family. Authentic table friendship is realized in communities that learn to overcome their differences for the sake of their unity in Christ (Galatians 3:28). Communion challenges believers to be of the same mind despite our differences (Philippians 2:2) and to find common ground in Christ, who binds us together in unity. The full potential of the Eucharist is realized not in isolation but in community, for the Lord's Supper transforms God's people from a group of self-seeking individuals into a vibrant community characterized by love for one another.

> *The Eucharist unites God's people to form communities in which we experience spiritual transformation by submitting to the hard work of relational reconciliation that being part of the body of Christ demands.*

Continuing Christ's Work of Redemption and Renewal

The church at Corinth was splitting apart at the seams. Its people had unfortunately become divided along socioeconomic lines. Romans 16:23 indicates that the Corinthian church met in a private home owned by a wealthy man named Gaius, whose house could accommodate anywhere from forty to sixty people. In the beginning, every time they met they enjoyed an actual meal together. Sadly though, the Corinthian congregation fell victim to the social mores of Greco-Roman culture and started giving preferential treatment to rich people at their gatherings. Wealthy members likely arrived early because their socioeconomic status allowed for more leisure time and greater flexibility in their schedules. As was customary at first-century Mediterranean banquets, these wealthy congregants were given prominent seats and larger portions of food and wine, which they likely consumed excessively. By contrast, slaves and day laborers had no control over their schedules since they were accountable to their masters and employers. Arriving later, slaves and manual laborers ate leftovers or missed out on the food entirely and were often seated in the hallway or courtyard, separated from the rest of the community. Instead of the ultimate expression of Christian unity, the Eucharist became a divisive event, prompting Paul's stinging rebuke that this was not the Lord's Supper they were eating (1 Corinthians 11:20). No matter what the Corinthian Christians were claiming to do, it was certainly not the Lord's Supper that they were celebrating when they met. The church at Corinth failed to understand the relationship between the meal and the sense of community that the meal represented. Paul essentially charges them with hypocrisy—gathering for the Lord's Supper like one big, happy family when they were anything but that.

Paul's warning about receiving the elements in an unworthy manner (1 Corinthians 11:27) was originally prompted by his concern for church unity, which in the case of the Corinthians was being undermined by their neglect of the poor and underprivileged. To partake of the bread and cup while at the same time sowing disunity in the church or neglecting the poor is to approach the Communion Table in an unsuitable fashion. Paul implores his flock at Corinth to discern the body of Christ whenever they eat the bread and drink the wine (1 Corinthians 11:29). "Body of Christ" is Christian shorthand for Jesus' ongoing presence in the world through his church. Partaking of the elements in remembrance of Christ brings to mind his sacrificial acts on behalf of humanity, which, in turn, motivates us to participate in Jesus' ongoing work of service to others. Communion invites God's people to discern how to act as the body of Christ in the world.

Moreover, the Eucharist guarantees that gratitude remains the proper motivation for a church's missional or outreach endeavors. As a result of breaking bread and eating together daily with grateful and generous hearts, the first Christians shared their resources with those in need (Acts 2:45-46). The Lord's Supper transforms ordinary worshipers into ambassadors of Christ (2 Corinthians 5:20) who emerge from the Table with hearts so filled with thanksgiving that they can't wait to share food and hospitality with those in need. Connecting acts of service to the Lord's Supper ensures that our benevolent actions aren't the product of human striving for God's approval or motivated by some misguided form of Christian triumphalism. Our third theological principle encompasses the global or mission-oriented dimensions of the Table: Communion calls grateful believers to continue Christ's transforming work of redemption and renewal by proclaiming the gospel both in word and deed.

Proclaim the gospel with words. Immediately after breaking bread with Jesus, the two Emmaus disciples returned to Jerusalem and boldly proclaimed the good news of the gospel: "The Lord has risen" (Luke 24:33-34). Several prominent theologians view the Eucharist as a "converting ordinance" because of its ability to articulate clearly the gospel message in a manner that invites a response. Where else in a typical church service is the salvation message more consistently announced or vividly displayed than in the sacrament of Communion? The Table is a simple but not simplistic proclamation of God's deliverance, a lucid reenactment of the death and resurrection of Jesus Christ. In addition to proclaiming the gospel message publicly, Communion emboldens each of us to share the good news of redemption with friends, loved ones, and acquaintances who do not yet know Christ.

Proclaim the gospel with deeds of humble service. The Lord's Supper challenges the people of God not only to share the gospel but also to live as agents of God's transforming grace. I believe that Paul instructs us to discern the body of Christ because our calling to be Jesus' hands and feet to a world in need can be expressed in a variety of ways. Christians must continually discern, as individuals and as churches, how to be the body of Christ in each of our specific settings. The Eucharist brings to mind all the times Jesus ate with sinners and society's castoffs and challenges us to stay attentive to the desperate cries of those who are suffering in our midst and throughout the world. Let's explore some of the ways Jesus' fellowship meals can motivate us to continue his ongoing work of redemption and renewal in the world.

Being the body of Christ means serving the poor. No doubt heeding Paul's concern for the poor, the early church received an offering after Communion that was distributed to needy members. As Justin Martyr describes:

> Those who are well-off and are willing give—each what he wishes according to his own choice—and what is gathered together is deposited with the president. And he assists orphans and widows and those who are in need because of illness or some other cause, and those who are in chains, and the foreigners who are staying with us.

Since the beginning of our faith, the grace Christians experience at the Table has translated into acts of benevolence on behalf of the poor and underresourced.

To observe Communion in remembrance of Christ means we follow the example he set during his earthly ministry and care for those who are sick and dying. Bringing Christ's healing presence to the world also challenges us to minister to those in need—to encourage those who are troubled, lonely, and disheartened; to help those who are weak and afflicted; and to exercise patience when confronted with people's short-comings (1 Thessalonians 5:14).

The Table galvanizes God's people to take a stand against injustice in the world and to stand in soli-darity with those who are impoverished, mar-ginalized, oppressed, and abused. The injustice that was inflicted on the Corinthian Christians who were poor and marginalized should remind us to stand up and advocate for those who are oppressed and to pray for those who are suf-fering persecution. May we remain ever mindful of justice issues in our own day.

The grace Christians experience at the Table has translated into acts of benevolence on behalf of the poor and underresourced.

Gordon Smith warns that if worshipers ne-glect our calling to minister to those in need, we miss one of the finer points of the sacrament:

> If participation in the Lord's Supper does not foster a capacity to see and act with courage, integrity, love, and justice in the world, then the holy meal is in danger of becoming nothing more than a form of communal self-indulgence. It must be an event that turns us back to a thoughtful and courageous engagement with the world.

Communion, therefore, enlists grateful believers to continue Christ's work of redemption and renewal through deeds of mercy and grace—to serve the poor, care for the sick, minister to those in need, and stand in solidarity with those who suffer injustice and oppression.

THE POWER OF A PIECE OF BREAD

Lewis Smedes marvels at how something as small and common as a piece of bread can be packed with such profound meaning for Christians:

The bread! Here in a simple staple of everyman's diet is the hope that man's tragedy will be overcome, his divisions healed, and the final peace and unity of mankind realized. The bread! It is Christ's magnificent gesture of confidence in his power to restore man to God and his fellows. A piece of bread, held in an ordinary sinner's hand and put in a forgiven man's mouth, holds the promise for the healing of mankind. . . . Brokenness is restored by bread—the bread which is Christ's body.

Smedes confirms that the Table is a dynamic catalyst for the private, social, and mission-oriented piety that epitomizes the three theological truths discussed in this chapter. As individuals we encounter Jesus at the Communion Table, receive forgiveness, and affirm our desire to live for him. Socially, the Lord's Supper shapes our relationships with those in the church by motivating us to reconcile disputes and allow our bond of unity in Christ to overcome our differences. The Eucharist cultivates a mission-oriented mindset by mobilizing us to proclaim the gospel by word and deed and to care for those who suffer. The spiritually formative properties of the Table are not meant merely for one's benefit but also for the sake of others. May we continue to realize and experience all the spiritually formative benefits that that little piece of sanctified bread and cup of wine have to offer us.

Reaping the Spiritual Benefits of the Lord's Supper in Your Setting

Given its potential for discipleship, I strongly urge churches intent on presenting every member fully mature in Christ (Colossians 1:28) to consider observing the Lord's Supper weekly if they do not already do so. The first generation of Christians broke bread together daily (Acts 2:46), although scholars are unclear about how widespread that was or how long that practice persisted. However, by the middle of the second century it is clear that weekly observances had become the norm. Offering the Eucharist less frequently than once a week does not represent traditional, historical church practice. Gathering around the Table occasionally instead of weekly deprives believers of the full range of its benefits.

Sometimes I hear leaders balk at the idea of weekly Communion fearing that doing so would cause the observance to eventually lose its meaning and become ritualized. However, no one ever expresses the same fear about any other part of the service. I've never heard anyone suggest that listening to a sermon every week or singing praise songs every Sunday would cause such things to lose their appeal. Besides, the Table need not be conducted the same way every time but can be practiced with a great deal of variety.

Four Biblically Based Ways to Celebrate the Table

In recent years scholars have taken the four different terms or characterizations of the Table found in Scripture as implying four different ways to experience the sacrament, each with its unique emphasis and tone. Though the names of all four categories are already familiar—Lord's Supper, Communion, Eucharist, and Heavenly Feast, the finer nuances of those names suggest a distinctive approach to each one.

Lord's Supper. The Table as Lord's Supper is based on 1 Corinthians 11:23-26, where Paul contemplates Jesus presiding over the Last Supper in the Upper Room. Christ presents the bread and cup to his disciples establishing a new covenant and instructs them henceforth to eat and drink in remembrance of him every time they gather. The Lord's Supper, the term commonly used in many Protestant churches, reminds worshipers that this sacred act is God's doing. Because it is God's Supper, God is the one who invites his people to come to his Table, which he has prepared for them, and God presides over the activity. Table observances in the spirit of the Lord's Supper focus on remembering the

suffering and death of Christ. As a result, they are always somber, re-
flective, and serious in tone; they may also include a time of confession.
Themes associated with the Lord's Supper include dying to self, taking
up one's cross, surrender, submission, doing God's will, and obedience.

Eucharist: Thanksgiving meal. The word *eucharist*, in the original
Greek, means "to give thanks" and is the most common term employed
by the early Christians to refer to their communal meal. The name is
derived from Jesus giving thanks before breaking bread (Matthew 26:27;
Mark 14:23; Luke 22:17, 19; 1 Corinthians 11:24), which is something
he habitually did before eating (Matthew 15:36; John 6:11, 23). The
New Testament church made a point to follow Jesus' example, always
stressing gratitude in the breaking of bread (Acts 27:35; Romans 14:6;
1 Corinthians 10:30; 14:16; 1 Timothy 4:3-4). If the term *eucharist*
sounds too Catholic for some Protestants, I recommend using Thanksgiving Meal instead, which still captures the spirit of the Eucharist. As
opposed to the Lord's Supper with its emphasis on Christ's crucifixion,
the Eucharist turns the spotlight on the resurrection, celebrating Jesus'
life, death, and resurrection and expressing gratitude for Christ's victory
over sin, death, and evil. The tone or feel is typically upbeat and joyous.

Communion: Family Meal. Another word commonly used for the
Table is *communion*, which, like all the other labels, has a distinct
meaning to it. Communion celebrates our fellowship with God and
with one another as made possible through Christ's sacrifice. Communion accentuates the communal nature of the Table. Some refer to
it as a Koinonia Celebration; I like to call it the Family Meal. The
biblical precedence for this type of celebration is found in 1 Corinthians 10:16-17, which connects our participation in the bread and cup
to our participation in the body of Christ. Insisting that there is one
bread and one body, Paul reasons that we who are many are one because we partake of the one bread. Many early writers developed
further the idea of grains of wheat or single grapes coming together to

form the Communion elements. Fourth-century theologian Augustine taught that

> bread doesn't come from a single grain, but from many. . . . And thus it is with wine. . . . Individual grapes hang together in a bunch, but the juice from them all is mingled to become a single brew. This is the image chosen by Christ our Lord to show how, at his own table, the mystery of our unity and peace is solemnly consecrated.

Communion expresses appreciation for our inclusion in God's family. The tone is typically warm and mellow. The emphasis in Communion is on God's people breaking bread together. Themes along the lines of love, unity, compassion, the body of Christ, and serving others fit well with a Communion-styled approach to the Table.

Heavenly Feast. A Table celebration known as Heavenly Feast or Heavenly Banquet is based on the lofty vision of the marriage supper of the Lamb (Revelation 19:6-10, 17-18) as well as Jesus' insistence that our eating and drinking proclaim his death until he comes (Matthew 26:29; 1 Corinthians 11:26). The Heavenly Feast essentially looks back to the death and resurrection of Christ but at the same time looks forward to his second coming. The mood it creates, therefore, is one of joyful anticipation, so the tone is celebratory, triumphant, and upbeat. Zac Hicks views the Table as an opportunity for worshipers to rehearse for that great wedding supper of the Lamb, "the party to end all parties, where everyone gets their fill and is drowned in joy."

Variety of methods. Our quick survey of the subtle differences in the meaning behind the various names associated with the Table reveals that there is more than one way to approach the sacrament. In other words, we don't have to observe the Table the same way every time; we can vary our approach. Constance Cherry likens the Table to a prism that we have to look at from different angles to fully appreciate the depth of its beauty; when churches glance at the prism from only one direction, they get stuck in a rut with only one way to approach this sacred act. The four methods outlined here—Lord's Supper, Eucharist (or Thanksgiving Meal), Communion (or Family Meal), and Heavenly Feast—are based on Scripture and offer a variety of meaningful and transforming encounters with Christ. Churches could employ the same liturgy every time or the Words of Institution for the sake of continuity but shape the opening comments, song selection, and prayer on that particular week's theme for the Table.

Connecting Word and Table

In addition to weekly practice I propose that the Table merits the kind of strategic service planning that enables the congregation to reap the spiritual benefits of the sacrament. Given the rich theology of the Table, it should not be difficult to establish some link between the sermon and Communion every week. The three theological truths permeating this chapter are not exhaustive by any means; they merely scratch the surface of the spiritual implications of the Lord's Supper. There's always some aspect of eucharistic theology that is relevant to the sermon.

Catholic writer Sister Heidi characterizes the Eucharist as "an always-new and ever-flowing source of strength for our life, source of hope, of jubilation, of joy, of festival . . . the most powerful life-giving reality enabling us to struggle against the powers of death and destruction." Rather than a perfunctory, one-dimensional ritual, the Table is a multivalent spiritual event with a wide variety of applications for personal piety.

10

LIVING IN OUR BAPTISM

ᘒᖆ

I RECENTLY SURVEYED THE COLLEGE STUDENTS in my spiritual formation classes to determine their impressions of baptism.
Nearly all of them shared that their baptism was a significant and meaningful experience, but it's not something they think about all that much.
As I probed further I couldn't help but notice that the students described
their experience of baptism as if it was a one-and-done occurrence—an
opportunity to give public witness of their commitment to Christ but
something they only had to do once to ensure going to heaven. None of
the students received in-depth instruction on the meaning of baptism;
about half of them attended a meeting beforehand, but most of the
meeting was spent discussing the logistics of the ceremony—what to
wear, how to proceed in and out of the baptismal area, and what to say.

I must admit that my students' assessment of baptism mirrors my
own experience. I too have fond memories of my baptism, but until I
studied the theology of the rite, I never thought of it as being relevant
to my life today; I suspect many Christians share similar sentiments. I've
never run across anyone who claimed that their baptism continues to
play a significant role in their ongoing spiritual formation. Compared to
Christian tradition, our modern view of baptism is narrow and woefully
incomplete. In the early church baptism was not only regarded as the

fundamental entry point into the body of Christ but also the beginning
of a person's formative, spiritual journey into the image of Christ. Paul
taught that in baptism we begin a new way of living (Romans 6:4). His
argument for Christians to live different from unbelievers hinges on the
fact that we are baptized people (Romans 6:3). From a biblical perspective, baptism not only signals the beginning of our new life in Christ
but also reveals insights on how to live that life day in and day out.

BAPTISM IN THE EARLY CHURCH

Early sources reveal that the New Testament church, in compliance with
the apostles' teaching, regarded baptism not merely as a one-time event
but as part of a long process of initiation into the Christian faith. The
original purpose of the *Didache* was to offer preparatory instruction on
the meaning of baptism. Central to its teaching is what the *Didache*
refers to as "The Two Ways" of life and death, which, based on Deuteronomy 30:19-20 and Psalms, pits the ways of God as opposed to Satan
and the ways of the world. God's way satisfies and generates life while
the devil's alternative is destructive and leads to death. The first generation of Christians was taught that their choice between God's way and
their way affected all aspects of their daily lives. Converts were warned
that living the Christian life involves making certain choices, that from
now on they would have to make a conscious effort to follow the Lord
instead of being pulled along by their natural tendencies. Additionally,
the *Didache* stipulated that every new believer has a spiritual mentor;
those being baptized and their mentors fasted for two days before the
baptism service. From the beginning of our faith, baptism represented
a serious commitment to follow Christ and was precipitated by dedicated teaching concerning basic Christian beliefs.

A third-century document known as *The Apostolic Tradition* reveals
that candidates for baptism at that time submitted to three years of study
known as the *catechumenate*, which, related to the English word

catechism, means "instruction." In the early church the process of becoming a Christian began with rigorous training, and induction into the faith became official when they were baptized. Even after their baptism, new inductees came to church every day for additional instruction on the meaning of the rite they had just experienced. This postbaptism instruction was called *mystagogy,* meaning "mysteries." The thinking was that a person did not fully understand and appreciate the finer nuances—the deeper mysteries—of baptism until they had experienced it. The purpose of the catechism was not to produce scholarly theologians but to help Christians develop godly character and virtuous lives. The teaching, therefore, was practical and easily accessible for all.

One of the unique features of both the catechumenate and the actual ceremony was the emphasis placed on the renunciations. During their baptism candidates were invited to renounce Satan and all his works. Since being baptized signified the desire to break free from sin and obey Christ, learning the art of renunciation helped those new in the faith to live obedient Christian lives in a pagan culture. The fact that the first believers were educated on the meaning of baptism both before and after being baptized and that it included coaching on how to conduct spiritual battle indicates that the sacrament has a wealth of wisdom to offer all Christians, no matter where they are in their spiritual development.

By the fourth century, Cyril, bishop of Jerusalem, was also overseeing a three-year study program that included robust theological study. Every day baptismal candidates gathered at the church at sunrise to sit under Cyril's teaching. A fourth-century nun named Egeria authored a famous account of a pilgrimage she took to Jerusalem during Lent and Holy Week. In Jerusalem she observed those early morning Bible studies with Cyril. Egeria describes the bishop sitting on a chair with the unbaptized gathered around him in a circle, and Cyril would go through the Scriptures, beginning with Genesis, and explain the literal and spiritual meaning of God's Word and answer questions. Like the churches represented by *The Apostolic Tradition* a century earlier, Cyril's church in Jerusalem also gave the renunciations a prominent role both in its preparatory teaching and in the rite of baptism. For Cyril, developing the habit of renouncing Satan and all his ways helped break one's bondage to sinful habits. The early church observed baptism in a way that reflected its essential role in Christian discipleship. For the founding matriarchs and patriarchs of the church, baptism was a one-time event whose value and significance lasted for a lifetime.

Living in Your Baptism as a Spiritual Practice

Martin Luther believed that baptism offers Christ-followers enough spiritually edifying material to study and put into practice for the rest of our lives. Luther was convinced that the spiritual implications of baptism were so vital that a Christian should say out loud every morning, "I am baptized." By encouraging believers to remember their baptism, Luther in effect calls us to look beyond the actual ritual, receive it as the "inexpressible treasure" that it is, and live out our baptism every day. Living in our baptism entails being continually renewed by our original commitment to follow Christ. If you were baptized as an infant or unaware of all it signified at the time, there is no need to be rebaptized. It doesn't matter when you were baptized or even how; what is important is that you live out the true meaning of baptism now.

Baptism is a landmark moment in a believer's life; it is an essential requirement for salvation (1 Peter 3:21). However, living like a baptized Christian is just as important as the experience of baptism itself. Remembering our baptism refreshes and rejuvenates believers by keeping us ever mindful of four spiritual realities that are indispensable for daily Christian living. Similar to our discussion of the Lord's Supper, this chapter will examine four theological truths that reveal baptism's inherently transforming potential: baptism empowers believers to live

(1) free from guilt and shame, (2) as those who are dead to sin but alive in Christ, (3) as God's beloved sons and daughters, and (4) according to the Holy Spirit.

Live free from guilt and shame. Baptism signifies that our sins have been washed away, that we are truly forgiven (Acts 22:16). On Pentecost, Peter instructed the people to repent and be baptized for the forgiveness of their sins (Acts 2:38). Baptism, in and of itself, does not confer forgiveness or guarantee salvation, for only Christ can cleanse us; baptism represents God's pledge, the seal of Christ's cleansing (Ephesians 5:26), which assures us of salvation and calls us to lives of faithful obedience. The writer of Hebrews teaches that the washing of our physical bodies with the pure water of the baptismal font underscores that we can draw near to God with the assurance that we've been cleansed completely from our sin (Hebrews 10:22). Baptism serves as a watershed moment in a Christian's spiritual journey (no pun intended). When we encounter doubts or uncertainties in our relationship with the Lord, we have tangible proof regarding our status before God; in something as ordinary and down-to-earth as water, we have the blessed assurance that we are forgiven of all our sins.

Many people are weighed down by guilt and shame. There's a sin or experience that constantly eats away at their self-respect and continually haunts them. John Calvin insists that even though we're baptized once, we are washed and purged for the rest of our lives. For those of us who struggle with guilt and shame, remembering our baptism ensures us that *all* our sins are forgiven. We are baptized. Therefore, we are set free from guilt and shame. We don't have to remain weighed down by self-contempt or paralyzed by self-disdain; the past is in the past. There truly is no condemnation for those

> *Living like a baptized Christian is just as important as the experience of baptism itself.*

of us who are in Christ (Romans 8:1). The redemption that Jesus brings is so complete that we've not only been delivered from the sins we've committed but also from all the hurt, evil, injustice, and abuse that others have inflicted on us. So we can put away any lingering sense of unworthiness, any nagging perfectionism, and all those negative voices from the past. Remembering our baptism sets us free from self-condemnation and self-loathing.

When we sin, Calvin encourages believers to remember our baptism and draw strength from it, fortifying our minds with the confidence that we are indeed forgiven of our sins. Though we often return to our baptism as weak and failed sinners, we find again God's promise of mercy, forgiveness, and grace. When we sin we often try to hide from God or avoid him, like Adam and Eve in the garden. Instead of running away from God, baptism invites us to run to God when we fail and let him comfort us, assure us of his forgiveness, and renew us in the Holy Spirit.

Live dead to sin but alive in Christ. To say that baptism is merely the outward sign of an inward cleansing from sin does not do justice to the New Testament's teaching on this topic. Martin Luther attests that it is

> indeed correct to say that Baptism is a washing away of sins, but the expression is too mild and weak to bring out the full significance of Baptism, which is rather a symbol of death and resurrection. . . . The sinner does not so much need to be washed as he needs to die, in order to be wholly renewed and made another creature, and to be conformed to the death and resurrection of Christ, with whom he dies and rises again through Baptism.

Luther is echoing Paul's use of baptism as a metaphor for our being baptized into Christ's death and raised to new life (Romans 6:3-4). Being submerged underwater represents our death to sin; coming up out of the water symbolizes our resurrection to new life.

Baptism for Paul is more than merely symbolic; it is a sacred act that unites us to Christ in his death and resurrection (Romans 6:5), enabling us to identify so deeply and thoroughly with the Son of God in his death and resurrection that we regard ourselves as being dead to sin and alive to God through Christ (Romans 6:11). Paul's concept of identifying with the death and resurrection of Christ goes far beyond mere, consenting head knowledge but empowers us to experience the freedom and benefits of Jesus' death and resurrection in our everyday lives. Those united with Christ in baptism participate in Jesus' death and his rising to new life here and now by continually dying to our old self and living as new people (2 Corinthians 5:17). Baptism is not merely a transaction that pronounces forgiveness for our sins; it unites us to Christ's death and resurrection in a way that sets us free from the power of sin and death, so that sin no longer has dominion over us. Baptism empowers Christians to live as dead-to-sin, alive-to-Christ people who are no longer captive to our destructive behavior, ungodly compulsions, and negative impulses.

To be dead to sin means that we keep offering up that old sinful nature of ours to be crucified with Christ so we are no longer controlled or enslaved by it (Romans 6:6). We abandon our self-serving and self-referenced way of being and living. Being dead to sin doesn't mean we no longer have sinful desires or encounter temptation but that we now have an alternative to sin; we don't have to be pulled into the ways of this world or controlled by our natural impulses. Even when it feels like our desires are raging out of control and about to drag us under, whatever sin we're contemplating is completely alien to who we truly are in Christ because we are dead to it. Living in our baptism as dead-to-sin people offers an alternative to sinful behavior.

Baptism unites us to Christ in his death so we can be united with him in his resurrection (Romans 6:5). Just as Christ was raised from the dead, we too are raised to live a new life, free from sin and death

(Romans 6:7). Since Jesus' resurrection seals his victory over sin and death, we too can experience victory over the spiritual deadness that holds us in bondage. Baptism signifies that the resurrection is more than just something to look forward to when we die; it represents a new way of living here and now. By enabling us to participate in Christ's resurrection, baptism empowers us to walk in freedom from sin and death.

By reminding us that we are dead to sin and alive in Christ, living in our baptism can help us make better choices when facing temptation. We can say no to sin because we are dead to it and yes to God because we are alive in Christ. Baptized believers cultivate a dead-to-sin, alive-to-Christ mindset for daily living.

Live as God's beloved son or daughter. The early Christians believed that everything that happened to Jesus can happen to us. Paul referred to Christ as the "firstfruits" (1 Corinthians 15:20-23), the "firstborn from among the dead" (Colossians 1:18), the first of many more to come who purpose to live as God intended human beings to live (Romans 8:29). Jesus' earthly life offers a preview of what's to come and what's possible for all who follow him. His baptism, for example, informed the first Christians regarding their own experience of this sacred ritual.

When Christ was baptized, he came up out of the Jordan River, and immediately the heavens opened (Mark 1:10). The Greek text indicates that the heavens did not part slowly and quietly but were forcefully torn open. The Gospel writer uses descriptive language to underscore the fact that at Jesus' baptism God the Father opened up the heavens and showered all of creation with precious gifts and invaluable blessings. The ancient church, believing that what happened to Jesus happens also to us, concluded that at Christian baptism God continues to open all of heaven and shower those being baptized with his love, grace, and favor.

This means that the same divine voice speaking at Jesus' baptism can also be heard at ours. In the same way that God the Father pronounced his love and approval of Jesus his Son, so at our baptism in Christ God looks on us with pleasure and delight and says, "You are my beloved son," or "You are my beloved daughter." Living in our baptism daily means that we receive those same words Jesus heard at his baptism as God's word to each of us personally. The most profound blessing accrued to baptized believers, according to Frederick Bruner, is that "we become as pleasing and as dear to the Father as the Father's very own Son, which is very dear indeed." Baptism invites those who have suffered terrible abandonment, neglect, or abuse from their earthly fathers or mothers to hear the voice of their good and gracious, eternal, heavenly Father, who loves them unconditionally. Baptism reminds us, through something as common and accessible as water, that we have been adopted into the family of God as his beloved sons and daughters (Ephesians 1:5; 1 John 3:1-2).

Living in our baptism also requires us, as members of God's family, to love all of God's other beloved children, including those that we find difficult to like, let alone love. First Corinthians 12:13 upholds that baptism forms God's people into one entity or body. Baptism, then, is an ongoing grace that invites each of us to live as God's beloved sons and daughters and to demonstrate unconditional love toward others.

Live according to the Spirit. As with the Lord's Supper, the Holy Spirit is once again the active agent in baptism, facilitating and mediating all the transforming benefits of the rite. However, baptism shares an especially unique relationship with the Holy Spirit, for baptism assures us of the Spirit's presence in our lives. When Jesus was baptized, the Spirit of God descended upon him like a dove (Matthew 3:16). Throughout the New Testament, baptism is directly connected to our receiving the Holy Spirit. We shouldn't presume, however, that baptism obligates God to confer the Holy Spirit, for that would make the Spirit subject to human action. Jesus taught that the Holy Spirit does not answer to our beck and call but is free as the wind that blows wherever it pleases (John 3:8). On the other hand, God promises to bestow his grace and Holy Spirit in baptism (Acts 2:38). However, we need to recognize that the Bible reveals a variety of ways that the Holy Spirit is imparted. From the book of Acts, for example, the Holy Spirit was given to the Samaritans after baptism (Acts 2:38; 8:15), to Cornelius before baptism (Acts 10:44-48), and to Paul and the Ephesians during baptism (Acts 9:17-18; Acts 19:5-6). Thus, how the Holy Spirit is conveyed cannot be predicted or manipulated, for it is entirely subject to God's providence. Though it is a mystery how and when the Spirit is imparted, baptism acts as a "seal"—a sign or indicator—assuring us of the Spirit's active presence in our lives (2 Corinthians 1:21-22). The Holy Spirit accomplishes in us and for us that which baptism signifies; the Spirit unites us to Christ, cleanses us from sin, and sanctifies us. In other words you don't need additional, supernatural experience to be "baptized in the Spirit." Christian baptism is in and of the Holy Spirit.

When I began teaching at a Christian Bible college, I was surprised that discussions about the Holy Spirit generated a fair amount of confusion and even anxiety among the students. Some were confused about the purpose of the Holy Spirit; others were concerned whether they were "filled with the Spirit." I discovered that many students questioned whether they were Spirit-filled because they didn't experience certain outward manifestations such as tongues, prophecy, word of knowledge, or some other supernatural demonstration. These young people did not grow up in Pentecostal or charismatic churches, yet their perception of the Spirit's presence was based on a visible, supernatural experience of it.

The Bible characterizes the Holy Spirit in a way that defies our stereotypical perception. First, the third member of the Trinity is quite the workhorse. Scripture refers to the Holy Spirit as our helper or advocate (John 14:16, 26; 15:26; 16:7) who teaches us (John 14:26; 1 Corinthians 2:13), reveals God's truth to us (1 Corinthians 2:10-11), convicts us of sin (John 16:8), leads and guides us (Acts 8:29; 13:2; 15:28), distributes spiritual gifts (1 Corinthians 12:11), intercedes in prayer for us (Romans 8:26-27), bears witness to and glorifies Christ (John 15:26; 16:14), and assures us that we've been adopted into God's family (Romans 8:9, 15-16; Galatians 4:6). The Holy Spirit does much on our behalf. Notice, however, that the Spirit's duties are more hidden and less sensationalized than we typically make out the work of the Spirit to be. Despite the occasional spectacle, like at Pentecost, the bulk of the Spirit's activities according to Scripture occurs behind the scenes. I'm not saying that the Spirit doesn't work supernaturally today because I believe he does. But these supernatural occurrences are not the only—and certainly not the predominant—manifestation of the Spirit. With a personality resembling that of an introvert, the Holy Spirit is a quiet activist, working in our lives and in the world in a manner that is more covert than overt.

The clandestine actions of the Holy Spirit are more supernatural in the long run than the Spirit's spontaneous, outward manifestations, because they prompt us to act in a way that goes against how we would naturally behave. Anytime our thoughts or affections turn to God, that is not our own doing, for we are not naturally inclined to seek God—his way of thinking and acting are completely foreign to us (Isaiah 55:8). Living a Spirit-filled life is unnatural and uncommon human behavior; it is contrary to our fallen nature (Galatians 5:17). Every time we think about God, are prompted to pray, or are bothered by our bad behavior—that's most likely the result of the Spirit indwelling us (1 Corinthians 3:16; 2 Timothy 1:14). The fruit of the Spirit represents God's ongoing work—again, undercover—to cultivate Christian character in our lives (Galatians 5:22-23). Thus, anytime we're moved to love someone difficult to love, experience peace amid turmoil, or show self-control or restraint, that is concrete evidence that the Holy Spirit is very much alive in us (Romans 8:11; Ephesians 5:18). Our baptism assures us that even though we may not always see the Spirit working, we are indeed filled with the Holy Spirit. To live in our baptism entails walking in the Spirit—staying in step with the Spirit's leading—daily (Galatians 5:25).

Living like baptized believers. Cyril of Jerusalem, who taught extensively on baptism, was so convinced of the spiritual benefits of this sacred ceremony that he considered it a great privilege to be baptized into the Christian faith. "Great indeed is the Baptism which is offered you," writes Cyril. "It is a ransom to captives; the remission of offenses; the death of sin; the regeneration of the soul; the garment of light; the holy seal indissoluble; the chariot to heaven; the luxury of paradise; a procuring of the kingdom; the gift of adoption." For Cyril, baptism is not the one-hit-wonder of the Christian faith that we've made it out to be. It is instead the theme song or soundtrack of the Christian life—a familiar tune that evokes a fond memory of the day we were baptized—that continues its beautiful melody for us to hear every day. In other words there is an ongoing spirituality to baptism that endures long after the ritual, and it is fundamentally transformational.

It is time for the modern church to rediscover what Christians through the ages have found to be true—that baptism offers valuable wisdom for daily Christian living. In the same way that our spiritual ancestors were called to live in their baptism, we too are called to live in ours and enjoy all the spiritual benefits of being baptized believers.

Make Baptism Memorable in Your Setting

I challenge churches today to make baptism memorable for those being baptized as well as those who witness the ceremony. Let's do everything we can to help new converts live as baptized believers and older Christians to remember their baptism. An obvious place to start is to offer instruction on the spiritual implications of baptism and to preach about it on Sunday morning from time to time.

We also need to make sure that we conduct baptism in a way that underscores its importance for the spiritual life. To that end, an increasing number of churches today are utilizing the public renunciations that the early Christians experienced. Liturgical churches already use the series of questions from the Book of Common Prayer, but now, many nonliturgical churches are either featuring those same questions or adapting them for their setting:

> *There is an ongoing spirituality to baptism that endures long after the ritual, and it is fundamentally transformational.*

Do you renounce Satan and all the spiritual forces of wickedness that rebel against God? If so, reply "I renounce them."

Do you renounce the evil powers of this world which corrupt and destroy the creatures of God? If so, reply "I renounce them."

Do you renounce all sinful desires that draw you from the love of God? If so, reply "I renounce them."

Do you turn to Jesus Christ and accept him as your Savior? If so, reply "I do."

Do you put your whole trust in his grace and love? If so, reply "I do."

Do you promise to follow and obey him as your Lord? If so, reply "I do."

If the verbiage is too formal for your church, feel free to come up with different wording that still captures the desire on the part of those being baptized to turn from sin and live in obedience to Christ.

While baptism is generally a time of commitment for new Christians, it can also serve as an opportunity for all believers to thank God for the gift of baptism in their own lives. Invite the congregation to pray for those newly baptized believers. Pray that they take their commitment to follow Christ seriously, that they read God's Word, learn how to pray, and grow in the faith. In other words, pray that they live in their baptism.

In addition to a formative approach to the observance, look for ways to weave the theme of baptism into your services. New Testament writers, especially Paul, habitually reference baptism or the idea of being a baptized believer as if they're purposely trying to remind us of our baptism. You too can help your people live in their baptism by referring to it in your comments or prayers. From time to time address them as baptized believers. The Nicene Creed is a wonderful addition to a service, especially a baptism service, because it acknowledges one baptism for the forgiveness of sins.

In recent days several well-known leaders in the evangelical community have renounced Christianity; they've taken to social media to proclaim publicly and loudly that they no longer uphold Christian values or follow Jesus. I can't help but wonder whether the way we conduct baptism—without any type of renunciation of sin and our former ways of living—has made it easier for people to renounce their Christian faith. Instead of reducing it to merely a public witness of the faith, we should offer our congregations a full-orbed baptism experience that is packed with a depth of meaning and provides spiritual guidance to our baptized members for the rest of their lives.

EPILOGUE

We Get to Do This!

⚜

THROUGHOUT MY LIFE I've enjoyed the privilege of planning and leading worship services with a team of people; for me, it's always been a group effort. Sometimes the process goes smoothly, ideas flow freely, and everything falls nicely into place. Other times the process is slow, tedious, and arduous, like pulling teeth. Despite the challenges, I often experience an adrenaline rush somewhere along the way when I'm struck with a deep appreciation for the opportunity to plan and lead worship for God's people. During a meeting or rehearsal I'll have a "pinch me, I can't believe this is real" moment and I feel like blurting out to everyone, "I can't believe we get to do this!" I have a hunch many of you have experienced the same thing.

Second Corinthians 3:18 evokes a similar emotion: "We all, who with unveiled faces contemplate the Lord's glory, are being transformed into his image with ever-increasing glory, which comes from the Lord, who is the Spirit." Paul is describing a communal experience—something "we all" do together—that transforms gathered worshipers into the image of Christ, who is the likeness of God (2 Corinthians 4:4). The impetus for this life-altering experience is that we contemplate,

behold, look at, or see the glory of the Lord, which is God's essence—
his nature or attributes. That, my friends, is what we do!

As worship planners and leaders we point people to Jesus; we help
them see who God really is. Some of those in the congregation will not
care to look; they come to church but keep everything and everyone at
a distance, including God. And we continue to pray for them. Others
look at Christ but then quickly turn away; they're distracted by busyness,
set in their ways, threatened by Jesus, not willing to give up control of
their lives to him. We pray for them too. Then some look at Jesus and
can't take their eyes off of him. They fixate on him, desire him, and
worship him. They take Jesus in and are forever changed. They keep
coming back to look at him, so they keep changing and keep growing
into the image of Christ. In each of these cases the responsibility for
transformation does not rest on our shoulders but on God's. God is the
one who redeems and renews people in Christ through the power of the
Holy Spirit. Our job is simply to point them to Jesus.

I hope this book helps you do an even better job of pointing your
people to Jesus every Sunday. Appendix four contains a series of questions based on the characteristics and distinctive features of transforming worship. The checklist-style questionnaire offers a basic
summary of each chapter of this book. Going through those questions
with your leadership team periodically will no doubt generate some
honest and hopefully constructive dialogue. More importantly, the list
can serve as a periodic checkup to keep your efforts aligned with a biblical perspective on worship.

What a wonderful privilege we have every Sunday to invite the people
of God to join us as we behold God in Christ, worship him for who he
is and all he's done, and then open ourselves up to his transforming work
in our lives. Praise God that we get to do this!

RESPONSIVE
SCRIPTURE READING

T HE FOLLOWING READING, drawn from Melanie Ross's book *Evangelical Versus Liturgical?* combines effectively Colossians 1–2 and Philippians 2.

LEADER. He is the image of the invisible God, the firstborn over all creation.

CONGREGATION. For by him all things were created: things in heaven and on earth, visible and invisible, whether thrones or powers or rulers or authorities; all things were created by him and for him.

LEADER. He is before all things, and in him all things hold together.

CONGREGATION. And he is the head of the body, the church; he is the beginning and the firstborn from among the dead so that in everything he might have the supremacy.

LEADER. God was pleased to have all his fullness dwell in him, and through him to reconcile to himself all things, whether things on earth or things in heaven, by making peace through his blood, shed on the cross. Therefore God exalted him to the highest place and gave him the name that is above every name.

CONGREGATION. That at the name of Jesus every knee should bow, in heaven and on earth and under the earth, and every tongue confess that Jesus Christ is Lord, to the glory of God the Father.

READERS' THEATER
SCRIPTURE READING

Christmas Worship

N OTE: This program is adapted by Rory Noland. No special costumes or staging is needed in a readers' theater presentation. Readers simply stand in place on the stage and read or speak their parts from memory. The following adaptation includes Scripture quotations from the English Standard Version of the Bible and contains reading parts for

Narrator 1	Shepherd 2
Narrator 2	Angel 1
Narrator 3	Host of Angels (group of 5-6)
Zechariah	Mary
Shepherd 1	

NARRATOR 1

Worship resounds throughout the Christmas story and for good reason. God became a man. He walked among us. Though Jesus Christ was in the form of God, he "did not count equality with God a thing to be grasped, but made himself nothing, taking the form of a servant, being born in the likeness of men" (Philippians 2:6-7).

NARRATOR 2

Those who witnessed the birth of Christ were more than just characters in a sentimental story. They were real people who took the time to notice the amazing things God was doing in the world around them.

They were so moved by what they saw, they couldn't help but overflow with passionate praise. Today we too take time to stop and remember anew the events leading up to the birth of our Lord and Savior, Jesus Christ, and we join those first Christmas worshipers in praise and adoration. We begin with Zechariah.

NARRATOR 3

An angel appeared to Zechariah with startling news. Zechariah's wife, Elizabeth, was to give birth to a son, and they were to name him John (better known to us today as John the Baptist). What made the news improbable was that Zechariah and Elizabeth were not a young couple. They were quite old, way past their child-bearing years. Because Zechariah scoffed at the angel's announcement, his vocal cords were stricken, and he was unable to speak until his son was born. Yet, at the birth of his son, the first words out of Zechariah's mouth were words of praise:

ZECHARIAH

"Blessed be the Lord God of Israel,
    for he has visited and redeemed his people
and has raised up a horn of salvation for us
    in the house of his servant David,
as he spoke by the mouth of his holy prophets from of old,
that we should be saved from our enemies
    and from the hand of all who hate us;
to show the mercy promised to our fathers
    and to remember his holy covenant,
the oath that he swore to our father Abraham, to grant us
    that we, being delivered from the hand of our enemies,
might serve him without fear,
    in holiness and righteousness before him all our days.
And you, child, will be called the prophet of the Most High;
    for you will go before the Lord to prepare his ways,

to give knowledge of salvation to his people
    in the forgiveness of their sins,
because of the tender mercy of our God,
    whereby the sunrise shall visit us from on high
to give light to those who sit in darkness and in the shadow of death,
    to guide our feet into the way of peace."

SHEPHERD 1

A bunch of us shepherds was out in the fields at night watching over our flocks. And out of nowhere this angel appeared. It was so bright we could hardly see and we were scared half to death—totally freaked out. Then the angel said,

ANGEL 1

"Fear not, for behold, I bring you good news of a great joy that will be for all the people. For unto you is born this day in the city of David a Savior, who is Christ the Lord. And this will be a sign for you: you will find a baby wrapped in swaddling cloths and lying in a manger."

SHEPHERD 2

Then suddenly an entire army of angels appeared saying,

HOST OF ANGELS

"Glory to God in the highest, and on earth peace among those with whom he is pleased!"

SHEPHERD 1

When the angels left, we looked at each other and said, "We gotta get to Bethlehem and check this thing out." So we left right away and found Mary and Joseph and the baby lying in a manger.

SHEPHERD 2

We told them everything that the angel had said to us. Then we went home glorifying and praising God for all we had seen and heard.

NARRATOR 1

Mary was just a teenager when an angel appeared to her with the news that she would bear a son—God's Son, one whose kingdom would know no end. Soon thereafter, she erupted into heartfelt praise and worship:

MARY

"My soul magnifies the Lord,
    and my spirit rejoices in God my Savior,
for he has looked on the humble estate of his servant.
    For behold, from now on all generations will call me blessed;
for he who is mighty has done great things for me,
    and holy is his name.
And his mercy is for those who fear him
    from generation to generation.
He has shown strength with his arm;
    he has scattered the proud in the thoughts of their hearts;
he has brought down the mighty from their thrones
    and exalted those of humble estate;
he has filled the hungry with good things,
    and the rich he has sent away empty.
He has helped his servant Israel,
    in remembrance of his mercy,
as he spoke to our fathers,
    to Abraham and to his offspring forever."

NARRATOR 2

In the same way that the Christmas story moved Zechariah, the shepherds, the angels, and Mary to worship God, the wise men "saw the child with Mary his mother, and they fell down and worshiped him."

ALL

Glory to God in the highest and on earth peace among those with whom he is pleased!

Corporate Prayer
of Confession

LEADER. Almighty God: you alone are good and holy. Purify our lives and make us brave disciples. We do not ask you to keep us safe, but to keep us loyal, so we may serve Jesus Christ, who was tempted in every way as we are, yet was faithful to you.

RESPONSE. Amen.

LEADER. From lack of reverence for truth and beauty; from a calculating or sentimental mind; from going along with mean and ugly things;

RESPONSE. O God, deliver us.

LEADER. From cowardice that dares not face truth; laziness content with half-truth; or arrogance that thinks we know it all;

RESPONSE. O God, deliver us.

LEADER. From artificial life and worship; from all that is hollow or insincere;

RESPONSE. O God, deliver us.

LEADER. From trite ideals and cheap pleasures; from mistaking hard vulgarity for humor;

RESPONSE. O God, deliver us.

LEADER. From being dull, pompous, or rude; from putting down our neighbors;

RESPONSE. O God, deliver us.

LEADER. From cynicism about others; from intolerance or cruel indifference;

RESPONSE. O God, deliver us.

LEADER. From being satisfied with things as they are, in the church or in the world; from failing to share your indignation about injustice;

RESPONSE. O God, deliver us.

LEADER. From selfishness, self-indulgence, or self-pity;

RESPONSE. O God, deliver us.

LEADER. From token concern for the poor, for lonely or loveless people; from confusing faith with good feeling, or love with wanting to be loved;

RESPONSE. O God, deliver us.

LEADER. For everything in us that may hide your light;

RESPONSE. O God, light of life, forgive us.

CHECKLIST FOR TRANSFORMING
WORSHIP SERVICES

T HE FOLLOWING CHECKLIST for worship planners also serves as a summary of the characteristics and distinctive features of a formative approach to worship as reflected in Scripture and practiced by the early church. See the designated chapters in *Transforming Worship* for detailed information regarding each question.

1. Do our services reflect a biblical understanding of how God desires to be worshiped (see chaps. 1-2)?

    - Do our services reflect the fact that gathered worship is a God-initiated meeting between the Lord and his people? Does the congregation understand that when we gather, God is the one calling us together, inviting us to encounter and experience him? (Exodus 24:1, 12; 25:1; Luke 24:15; John 4:23-24)

    - Do our services reflect the fact that worship is by nature dialogical? Do our people perceive that the service is essentially an interactive meeting in which God speaks, we listen, and then respond to the Lord? (Exodus 24:3; Luke 24:17-27)

    - Do our services boldly and consistently proclaim who God is and what God has done? (Exodus 15; Psalm 145:5; Luke 24:34-35; 1 Peter 2:9)

    - Do our services give expression to our covenant relationship with God? Do we consistently allow people to express, renew, or reaffirm their commitment to follow Christ? (Exodus 24:3, 7; Luke 22:20; 24:27)

- Do our services consistently reenact God's saving acts of redemption? Does the manner in which we observe the Lord's Supper and baptism reinforce the spiritual implications of these sacred acts? (Exodus 24:4-5; Luke 24:30-31)

- Are our services Christocentric? Is it clear to our people that we worship Jesus Christ as Lord and Savior? (Luke 24:34; Revelation 5:8-13)

- Is our worship trinitarian? Do we pray to each of the three persons of the Trinity and glorify God the Father, God the Son, and God the Holy Spirit?

2. Do our services follow the basic template for worship outlined in Scripture that the early church embraced as its general order of service (see chap. 2)?

- Does the manner in which we start our services effectively establish that God is calling us together to worship? (Psalms 96–101)

- Does the worship set focus on the Lord? Does it proclaim who God is and celebrate all he has done? Does it consistently highlight the attributes of God and God's marvelous deeds? (Exodus 15; Psalm 145:5; 1 Peter 2:9)

- Do we allow the Word of God to speak to us at various points during the service or only in the sermon? (Acts 2:42; 2 Timothy 3:16-17; Romans 12:2)

- Do we practice weekly Communion or offer the congregation some meaningful way to respond to the sermon? (Acts 2:42, 46)

- Do we send people out with a meaningful charge or blessing? (Numbers 6:24-26; Matthew 28:19-20)

3. Do our services adequately edify believers and evangelize unbelievers (see chap. 3)?

- Do we address the spiritual needs of believers as a prime priority and the needs of unbelievers as a secondary priority?

- Do our services seek to edify believers by pointing them to Christ? (1 Corinthians 14:3-5, 12, 17, 23, 26; Romans 14:19)

- Do we strive to make unbelievers feel welcome at church?

- Do we as leaders and as a church worship boldly, unapologetically, and passionately as a witness to the nations? (2 Samuel 22:50; Psalm 18:49; Matthew 22:37)

- Do we address seekers during the service and help them understand what's going on in the service or why we do what we do? (1 Corinthians 14:9, 16, 24)

- Do we talk about and present a complete picture of conversion that includes spiritual formation? (John 3:3-5; Romans 6:4; 8:29; 2 Corinthians 5:17-18; Titus 3:5; 1 Peter 2:2)

4. Do we follow historic church practice and approach Sunday morning like it's our church's primary, formative event? If so, how? If not, how should we go about doing that in our setting (see chap. 4)?

5. Are there any Christian symbols we use regularly that need to be explained?

- Do our people fully understand the rituals or routines associated with Sunday morning?

- Does our service do an adequate job of conveying the sacredness of worship?

- Are there any changes we need to make in these areas?

- Do our worship services promote or convey God's transcendence along with his immanence? If so, how? If not, how can we accomplish that for our congregation? (Hebrews 12:28; Acts 17:27; Revelation 3:20; see chap. 5)

6. Do we allow the congregation to participate in prayer (see chap. 6)?

   • Do we give our worshipers ample opportunity to pray?

   • Do our prayers on Sunday morning consistently include thanksgiving and intercessory prayers?

   • Do we expose our people to both scripted and spontaneous prayers?

7. Do we consistently present Scripture readings throughout the service or only in the sermon (see chap. 7)?

   • Do we present Scripture with the preparation and forethought it deserves? Do we read it with passion and energy? Do we read it like we love it?

   • Do we present Scripture at times in fresh and creative ways?

8. Do our services include a regular time of corporate confession (see chap. 8)?

9. Do we observe the Lord's Supper with enough regularity, variety, and forethought so our people can experience all the spiritual benefits it has to offer (see chap. 9)?

10. Do we conduct baptism in a way that underscores its ongoing significance for the spiritual life? Do our people know what it means to live in their baptisms (see chap. 10)?

NOTES

INTRODUCTION: WHAT IS TRANSFORMING WORSHIP?

11 Transforming *worship draws from*: Because churches differ on how they refer to the sacrament of the Lord's Supper, I will use the terms *Communion, Eucharist, Lord's Supper*, and *Table* interchangeably throughout this book.

12 *Allen Ross offers a compelling vision*: Allen P. Ross, *Recalling the Hope of Glory: Biblical Worship from the Garden to the New Creation* (Grand Rapids, MI: Kregel, 2006), 39.

13 *Gregory Jones laments*: L. Gregory Jones, "Beliefs, Desires, Practices, and the Ends of Theological Education," in *Practicing Theology: Beliefs and Practices in Christian Life* (Grand Rapids, MI: Eerdmans, 2002), 190.

14 *Jones further observes*: Jones, "Beliefs, Desires, Practices," 192.

1 IT ALL STARTED AT SINAI

19 *God brought Israel to Sinai*: Samuel E. Balentine, *The Torah's Vision of Worship* (Minneapolis: Fortress Press, 1999), 126-27.

20 *Participants were either sprinkled*: Janice R. Leonard, "The Covenant Basis of Biblical Worship," in *The Biblical Foundations of Christian Worship*, ed. Robert E. Webber, *The Complete Library of Christian Worship* (Nashville: StarSong, 1994), 1:57.

   Covenant partners sometimes shared a meal: Leonard, "Covenant Basis of Biblical Worship," 57.

21 *Atop Sinai, Israel's leaders*: Commentators agree that these leaders did not actually see God face-to-face, for no one can see God and live (Exodus 33:20). According to the text, the men described seeing God's feet. Durham concludes that Moses and his companions experienced a theophany or manifestation of God's presence. See John I. Durham, *Exodus*, Word Bible Commentary (Waco, TX: Word, 1987), 344.

22 *Though Israel emerged from slavery*: Balentine, *The Torah's Vision of Worship*, 65.

   Robbie Castleman maintains: Robbie F. Castleman, *Story-Shaped Worship: Following Patterns from the Bible and History* (Downers Grove, IL: IVP Academic, 2013), 42.

22   *The foundational principles listed*: Constance M. Cherry, *The Worship Architect: A Blueprint for Designing Culturally Relevant and Biblically Faithful Services* (Grand Rapids, MI: Baker Academic, 2010).

23   *Constance Cherry emphasizes*: Constance M. Cherry, *The Worship Architect: A Blueprint for Designing Culturally Relevant and Biblically Faithful Services* (Grand Rapids, MI: Baker Academic, 2010), 45.

25   *Israel's worship was designed*: Castleman, *Story-Shaped Worship*, 42.

2 Updating the Ancient Formula for Sunday Services

30   *Historians report that the early church*: See for example Paul F. Bradshaw, *The Search for the Origins of Christian Worship: Sources and Methods for the Study of Early Liturgy* (New York: Oxford University Press, 2002), 52-53.

The Emmaus narrative confirms: I am indebted to Constance Cherry for her excellent exegesis of the Emmaus story, especially her insights on worship as a transformational journey. See Cherry, *The Worship Architect: A Blueprint for Designing Culturally Relevant and Biblically Faithful Services* (Grand Rapids, MI: Baker Academic, 2010), 15-17.

32   *Robert Webber is among the many scholars*: Robert E. Webber, *Ancient-Future Time: Forming Spirituality Through the Christian Year* (Grand Rapids, MI: Baker Books, 2004), 152.

Constance Cherry effectively links: Cherry, *Worship Architect*, 47-48.

33   *At first, a twofold worship order*: Constance M. Cherry, *Worship Architect*, 46.

The earliest believers: Bernard Cooke and Gary Macy, *Christian Symbol and Ritual: An Introduction* (New York: Oxford University Press, 2005), 94.

History's first Jews for Jesus: Cooke and Macy, *Christian Symbol and Ritual*, 94.

Following the Emmaus model: Arthur A. Just, *The Ongoing Feast: Table Fellowship and Eschatology at Emmaus* (Collegeville, MN: Liturgical Press, 1993), 139.

Two additional components: Cherry, *Worship Architect*, 46.

By the third century the fourfold worship service: Greg Scheer, *Essential Worship: A Handbook for Leaders* (Grand Rapids, MI: Baker Books, 2016), 80.

34   *An effective call to worship*: Robert Webber, *Planning Blended Worship: The Creative Mixture of Old and New* (Nashville: Abingdon, 1998), 51.

The Book of Common Worship *contains a rich collection*: *Book of Common Worship* (Louisville, KY: Westminster John Knox, 1993), 12.

36   *The sending is more than a signal*: Clayton J. Schmit, *Sent and Gathered: A Worship Manual for the Missional Church* (Grand Rapids, MI: Baker Academic, 2009), 47.

36 *Rather than the end*: Robert E. Webber, *Worship Is a Verb: Eight Principles for Transforming Worship* (Peabody, MA: Hendrickson, 1992), 102.

38 *Reflecting the evangelistic fervor of the day*: Charles Finney, quoted in Melanie C. Ross, *Evangelical Versus Liturgical? Defying a Dichotomy* (Grand Rapids, MI: Eerdmans, 2014), 14.

    Finney and company adopted: The following explanation of Finney's threefold strategy is based on Ross, *Evangelical Versus Liturgical?*, 14-15.

39 *Reflecting the American proclivity*: James F. White, *Documents of Christian Worship: Descriptive and Interpretive Resources* (Louisville, KY: Westminster John Knox, 1992), 114.

    His insistence that God did not establish: White, *Documents of Christian Worship*, 115.

    In his later years Finney: Scot McKnight, *The King Jesus Gospel: The Original Good News Revisited* (Grand Rapids, MI: Zondervan, 2016), 85.

    Finney's three-pronged structure: Scheer, *Essential Worship*, 67-68.

41 *the Table reenacts God's saving act*: I use the term *Table* here, but feel free to refer to this segment as Communion, Eucharist, or Lord's Supper if that term is more appropriate or suitable for your setting.

3 How to Edify Believers and Evangelize Unbelievers

48 *this paradigm favors "event evangelism"*: The term arena evangelism has also been used.

49 *A four-year research project chronicled*: Greg L. Hawkins and Cally Parkinson, *Reveal: Where Are You?* (South Barrington, IL: Willow Creek Association, 2007).

50 *Timothy Keller lists several characteristics*: Timothy Keller, "Evangelistic Worship," *Gospel in Life.com*, accessed June 28, 2018, 3, https://static1.squarespace.com /static/5315f2e5e4b04a00bc148f24/t/537a726be4b0d45559686db1 /1400533611277/Evangelistic_Worship.pdf.

53 *they were not seeker-sensitive*: Alan Kreider, *The Patient Ferment of the Early Church: The Improbable Rise of Christianity in the Roman Empire* (Grand Rapids, MI: Baker Academic, 2016), 11, 14. Kreider reports that after Nero began systematically persecuting Christians in AD 68, "churches around the empire—at varying speeds in varying places—closed their doors to outsiders" (11).

55 *It's a vicious cycle*: Keller, "Evangelistic Worship," 6.

56 *When we continually worship*: Keller, "Evangelistic Worship," 6.

59 *Martin Luther taught that our life*: Martin Luther, "An Argument in Defense of All the Articles of Dr. Martin Luther Wrongly Condemned in the Roman Bull

(1521)," trans. Charles M. Jacobs, in *Works of Martin Luther* (Philadelphia: Muhlenberg Press, 1930), 3:31.

59   *salvation is not merely*: Ruth Barton, *Life Together in Christ: Experiencing Transformation in Community* (Downers Grove, IL: InterVarsity Press, 2014), 11.

4 RECLAIMING SUNDAY MORNING AS THE
CHURCH'S PRIMARY, FORMATIVE EVENT

61   *Kreider proposes that the values*: Alan Kreider, *The Patient Ferment of the Early Church: The Improbable Rise of Christianity in the Roman Empire* (Grand Rapids, MI: Baker Academic, 2016), 135.

a first-century discipleship manual: Didache 16.2, in Aaron Milavec, *The Didache: Text, Translation, Analysis and Commentary* (Collegeville, MN: Liturgical Press, 2003).

Even a cursory glance: See, for example, the writings, homilies, or sermons of Origen, Irenaeus, Basil of Caesarea, Athanasius of Alexandria, John Chrysostom, Cyril of Jerusalem, and Augustine of Hippo.

the church's first theologians: Ellen T. Charry, *By the Renewing of Your Minds: The Pastoral Function of Christian Doctrine* (New York: Oxford University Press, 1997), 85.

62   *Sermons at this time were brief*: Kreider, *Patient Ferment of the Early Church*, 197.

Tertullian speaks of church members reading: Tertullian, *Apology* 39.3, trans. T. R. Glover, Loeb Classical Library (Cambridge: Harvard University Press, 1931), 175. Tertullian referred to this teaching as *disciplina praeceptorum*, Latin for "disciplines of the precepts." See Kreider, *Patient Ferment of the Early Church*, 57.

"Christians are made, not born": Tertullian, *Apology* 18.4.

After the Scripture reading: Justin Martyr, *The First Apology* 67, trans. Thomas B. Falls, Fathers of the Church (New York: Christian Heritage, 1948), 106-7.

63   *Christianity's liturgical tradition is based*: Susan J. White, *The Spirit of Worship: The Liturgical Tradition* (Maryknoll, NY: Orbis, 2000), 15.

64   *In the first, Christ was our redemption*: Bernard of Clairvaux, *Sermo 5, In Adventu Domini 1-3*, cited in Paul F. Bradshaw and Maxwell E. Johnson, *The Origins of Feasts, Fasts and Seasons in Early Christianity* (Collegeville, MN: Liturgical Press, 2011), 166.

66   *Robert Webber affirms*: Robert E. Webber, *Worship Is a Verb: Eight Principles for Transforming Worship* (Peabody, MA: Hendrickson, 1992), 161.

By inviting believers to: Webber, *Worship Is a Verb*, 161.

67   *Christians act morally or ethically*: Maxwell Johnson, *Praying and Believing in Early Christianity: The Interplay Between Christian Worship and Doctrine* (Collegeville, MN: Liturgical Press, 2013), 98.

      Mike Cosper insists that our worship: Mike Cosper, *Rhythms of Grace: How the Church's Worship Tells the Story of the Gospel* (Wheaton, IL: Crossway, 2013), 94.

      Robert Mulholland describes these spiritual disciplines: M. Robert Mulholland Jr., *Invitation to a Journey: A Road Map for Spiritual Formation* (Downers Grove, IL: InterVarsity Press, 1993), 103.

68   *human beings are defined by*: James K. A. Smith, *Desiring the Kingdom: Worship, Worldview, and Cultural Formation* (Grand Rapids, MI: Baker Academic, 2009), 47-51.

      This love or desire is aimed: Smith, *Desiring the Kingdom*, 51.

      our desires get aimed in specific directions: Smith, *Desiring the Kingdom*, 82-85.

      Our most influential routines: Smith, *Desiring the Kingdom*, 58.

      We are complex, embodied people: Smith, *Desiring the Kingdom*, 60.

71   *Emphasize the spiritual dimension*: For more ideas on how to incorporate the lectionary and the Christian Year into services, see Robert E. Webber, *Ancient-Future Time: Forming Spirituality Through the Christian Year* (Grand Rapids, MI: Baker Books, 2004); Philip Pfatteicher, *Journey into the Heart of God: Living the Liturgical Year* (New York: Oxford University Press, 2013); Hoyt L. Hickman, Don E. Saliers, Laurence Hull Stookey, and James F. White, *The New Handbook of the Christian Year* (Nashville: Abingdon Press, 1992); White, *Spirit of Worship*; and David A. deSilva, *Sacramental Life: Spiritual Formation Through the Book of Common Prayer* (Downers Grove, IL: InterVarsity Press, 2008).

5 Recovering a Sense of the Sacred in Modern Worship

72   *Such narrow-mindedness is ironic*: John Calvin, *Institutes of the Christian Religion* 4.14.3, ed. John T. McNeill, trans. Ford Lewis Battles (Philadelphia: Westminster Press, 1960).

      our faith is "slight and feeble": Calvin, *Institutes* 4.14.3.

73   *God instituted Israel's system*: For a detailed explanation of the various types of Old Testament sacrifices and their meanings, see Tremper Longman, *Immanuel in Our Place: Seeing Christ in Israel's Worship* (Phillipsburg, NJ: P&R, 2001), chaps. 7–9.

75   *Janine Morgan finds that rituals*: Janine Paden Morgan, "Emerging Eucharist: 'This Is His Story, This Is My Song,'" *Missiology* 39, no. 4 (October 2011): 446.

75   *During times of tragedy or turmoil*: Morgan, "Emerging Eucharist," 447.

    ritual can no longer be considered: Timothy D. Son, *Ritual Practices in Congregational Identity Formation* (New York: Lexington Books, 2014), 68.

76   *People attach meaning to certain symbols*: Gordon T. Smith, *A Holy Meal: The Lord's Supper in the Life of the Church* (Grand Rapids, MI: Baker Academic, 2005), 21.

77   *sacraments are more than merely a sign*: Calvin, *Institutes* 4.17.3.

78   *the early church considered any object*: Bernard Cooke and Gary Macy, *Christian Symbol and Ritual: An Introduction* (New York: Oxford University Press, 2005), 37.

    the divine presence could be uniquely: Cooke and Macy, *Christian Symbol and Ritual*, 38-39.

79   *revivalists sought new measures*: John D. Witvliet, *Worship Seeking Understanding: Windows into Christian Practice* (Grand Rapids, MI: Baker Books, 2003), 171.

    With the sign of God's presence: Witvliet, *Worship Seeking Understanding*, 171-72.

80   *since God is enthroned on the praises*: For an excellent and thorough analysis of the sacramentality of contemporary worship, see Swee Hong Lee and Lester Ruth, *Lovin' on Jesus: A Concise History of Contemporary Worship* (Nashville: Abingdon Press, 2017), 124-39.

    worship music has taken on sacramental overtones: Witvliet, *Worship Seeking Understanding*, 233.

83   *a new era in sacramental theology*: James F. White, *Documents of Christian Worship: Descriptive and Interpretive Resources* (Louisville, KY: Westminster John Knox, 1992), 142.

    Edward Schillebeeckx as a leading voice: White, *Documents of Christian Worship*, 142.

    Jesus is the utmost "primordial sacrament": Edward Schillebeeckx, *Christ the Sacrament of the Encounter with God* (New York: Sheed & Ward, 1963), 15.

    As the personal, intimate manifestation: Schillebeeckx, *Christ the Sacrament of the Encounter*, 15.

    Sacraments are not things but encounters: Schillebeeckx, *Christ the Sacrament of the Encounter*, 44.

    gathered worship offers sacramental realities: Michael Baggot, "The Digital Triptych: Virtual and Sacramental Reality," *First Things*, August 19, 2016, www.firstthings.com/blogs/firstthoughts/2016/08/the-digital-triptych.

6 LET US PRAY!

93   *Psalm 55:17 confirms*: The prophet Daniel got down on his knees three times every day even though he knew he could be killed for praying in public (Daniel 6:6-12).

     this Jewish prayer regimen carried over: Aaron Milavec, *The Didache: Text, Translation, Analysis and Commentary* (Collegeville, MN: Liturgical Press, 2003), 65.

     Christianity's earliest thinkers wrote: Alan Kreider, *The Patient Ferment of the Early Church: The Improbable Rise of Christianity in the Roman Empire* (Grand Rapids, MI: Baker Academic, 2016), 204.

     waging spiritual warfare against sickness: Clement of Alexandria, "The Rich Man's Salvation," *Quis dives salvetur* 34, trans. G. W. Butterworth, Loeb Classical Library (Cambridge: Harvard University Press, 1919), 343.

     prayer a source of unlimited power: Origen, *Contra Celsum* 8.73, trans. Henry Chadwick (New York: Cambridge University Press, 1953), 509.

     Justin Martyr depicts worshipers: Justin Martyr, *First Apology* 65, ed. and trans. Edward Rochie Hardy, Early Christian Fathers (New York: Macmillan, 1970), 285.

     Ancient Christians typically prayed standing: Kreider, *Patient Ferment of the Early Church*, 204-5.

     Origen allowed those with physical ailments: Origen, *Prayer* 31.2, trans. John J. O'Meara, Ancient Christian Writers 19 (New York: Newman Press, 1954), 131.

94   *some leaders encouraged worshipers to pray*: Kreider, *Patient Ferment of the Early Church*, 205.

     Early believers prayed mightily: Kreider, *Patient Ferment of the Early Church*, 205.

     prayers as "gutsy" and "passionate": Kreider, *Patient Ferment of the Early Church*, 207.

     belonged to the people: Robert E. Webber, *Worship Is a Verb: Eight Principles for Transforming Worship* (Peabody, MA: Hendrickson, 1992), 145.

95   *the major prayer of the service*: Hughes Oliphant Old, *Leading in Prayer: A Workbook for Worship* (Grand Rapids, MI: Eerdmans, 1995), 176.

     prominent petition on the minds of early church: See Romans 15:5-6, 13; 2 Corinthians 13:7; Ephesians 3:16-19; 6:18; 1 Thessalonians 3:10-13; 5:23; 2 Thessalonians 2:16-17; 3:5, 16; Hebrews 13:21.

96   *Tertullian reports that the churches*: Tertullian, *Apology* 39.2, trans. T. R. Glover, Loeb Classical Library (Cambridge: Harvard University Press, 1931), 175.

     By the fourth century most churches: Old, *Leading in Prayer*, 177-78.

     Early Christian gatherings typically featured: Old, *Leading in Prayer*, 178.

96   *The service included prayers for church leaders*: Old, *Leading in Prayer*, 178.

     They also prayed for the emperor: Old, *Leading in Prayer*, 178.

97   *Old distinguishes the two*: Old, *Leading in Prayer*, 291.

     Hebrew verb barak: Willem A. VanGemeren, ed., *New International Dictionary of Old Testament Theology and Exegesis* (Grand Rapids, MI: Zondervan, 1997), 1:764.

     We bless God because: VanGemeren, *New International Dictionary of Old Testament Theology*, 764.

     first Christians remained committed to "the prayers": Though missing in some translations, the original Greek includes the definite article here.

98   *Lord's Prayer as a divine gift*: Milavec, *Didache*, 65.

     The extensive use of plural pronouns: Milavec, *Didache*, 65.

     Didache *recommends that Christians recite*: *Didache* 8.3.

     praying in a perfunctory manner: *Didache* 8.2.

     Rabbis were known for encouraging: Milavec, *Didache*, 66-67.

99   *the* Didache *urged believers to gather*: Milavec, *Didache*, 67.

     Christians expounded extemporaneously: Milavec, *Didache*, 67.

100 *the Holy Spirit is always at work*: Constance M. Cherry, *The Worship Architect: A Blueprint for Designing Culturally Relevant and Biblically Faithful Services* (Grand Rapids, MI: Baker Academic, 2010), 41.

     Though the Holy Spirit may appear: Cherry, *Worship Architect*, 41.

     It is presumptuous, therefore: Cherry, *Worship Architect*, 41.

102 *Jesus takes us with him*: James B. Torrance, "Prayer and the Priesthood of Christ," in *A Passion for Christ: The Vision That Ignites Ministry* (Lenoir, NC: PLC Publications, 1999), 58.

     Jesus takes our prayers: James B. Torrance, *Worship, Community and the Triune God of Grace* (Downers Grove, IL: InterVarsity Press, 1996), 46.

103 *We can only pray in the name*: Torrance, "Prayer and the Priesthood of Christ," 56.

     corporate prayer opens the windows: Dirk G. Lange, "A Baptismal Example: Communal Prayer and the Missional Church," in *Cultivating Sent Communities: Missional Spiritual Formation*, ed. Dwight J. Zscheile (Grand Rapids, MI: Eerdmans, 2012), 201.

104 *Whenever Christians assemble*: Torrance, *Worship, Community and the Triune God of Grace*, 14.

105   *train Christians to pray Monday*: Zac Hicks, *The Worship Pastor: A Call to Ministry for Worship Leaders and Teams* (Grand Rapids, MI: Zondervan, 2016), 61.

106   *Have your congregation pray*: Old, *Leading in Prayer*, 175.

      Intercede faithfully for those suffering: Lukas Vischer, *Intercession* (Eugene, OR: Wipf & Stock, 1980), 62.

      Scot McKnight commends both: Scot McKnight, *The King Jesus Gospel: The Original Good News Revisited* (Grand Rapids, MI: Zondervan, 2016), 175-76.

107   *great hymnals and prayer books*: I have used or adapted prayers from the following sources, all are highly recommended: *The Book of Common Prayer*; *The Book of Common Worship*; Arthur Bennett, ed., *The Valley of Vision: A Collection of Puritan Prayers and Devotionals* (Edinburgh, Scotland: Banner of Truth, 1975); Hughes Oliphant Old, *Leading in Prayer: A Workbook for Worship* (Grand Rapids, MI: Eerdmans, 1995); *Celtic Daily Prayer* (Morpeth, UK: Northumbria Community, 2000); *The Iona Abbey Worship Book* (Glasgow, Scotland: Wild Goose, 2001). Another excellent source is Hoyt L. Hickman, Don E. Saliers, Laurence Hull Stookey, and James F. White, *The New Handbook of the Christian Year* (Nashville: Abingdon Press, 1992).

7 Engaging the Preached and Unpreached Word of God

109   *By the first century it was customary*: Bernard Cooke and Gary Macy, *Christian Symbol and Ritual: An Introduction* (New York: Oxford University Press, 2005), 94.

110   *reading the memoirs of the apostles*: Justin Martyr, *First Apology* 65, ed. and trans. Edward Rochie Hardy, *Early Christian Fathers* (New York: Macmillan, 1970), 287.

111   *only 5 percent of the populous*: David Rhoads, "What is Performance Criticism?" in *The Bible in Ancient and Modern Media: Story and Performance*, ed. Holly E. Hebron and Philip Ruge-Jones (Eugene: Cascade Books, 2009), 84-85.

      bunch of words waiting to be spoken: Whitney Shiner, "Oral Performance in the New Testament World," in *The Bible in Ancient and Modern Media: Story and Performance*, ed. Holly E. Hebron and Philip Ruge-Jones (Eugene, OR: Cascade Books, 2009), 49.

      The earliest Christian authors wrote: Max McLean and Warren Bird, *Unleashing the Word* (Grand Rapids, MI: Zondervan, 2009), 47.

112   *readers portrayed characters and express emotion*: Richard F. Ward and David J. Trobisch, *Bringing the Word to Life: Engaging the New Testament Through Performing It* (Grand Rapids, MI: Eerdmans, 2013), 23.

      heard only a portion of the writings: Rhoads, "What Is Performance Criticism?" 84.

112   *Scripture reading done from memory*: Shiner, "Oral Performance in the New Testament World," 53.

      the unwieldy nature of ancient scrolls: Shiner, "Oral Performance in the New Testament World," 52.

113   *no punctuation or capitalization*: Ward and Trobisch, *Bringing the Word to Life*, 28.

114   *Having someone verbalize the text*: John P. Burgess, *Why Scripture Matters: Reading the Bible in a Time of Church Conflict* (Louisville, KY: Westminster John Knox, 1998), 59-60.

      encounter with Scripture as a dynamic experience: Burgess, *Why Scripture Matters*, 59-60.

      soaking oneself in Scripture: N. T. Wright, *After You Believe: Why Christian Character Matters* (New York: HarperCollins, 2010), 261.

      The practice of lectio divina: David G. Benner, *Opening to God: Lectio Divina and Life as Prayer* (Downers Grove, IL: InterVarsity Press, 2010), 47.

      approached the Torah from two distinct: Benner, *Opening to God*, 47.

115   *Third-century scholar Origen utilized*: Benner, *Opening to God*, 47-48.

      Saint Benedict established lectio divina: Benner, *Opening to God*, 48.

      Lectio fosters the expectation: Christopher A. Hall, "Reading Christ into the Heart: The Theological Foundations of *Lectio Divina*," in *Life in the Spirit: Spiritual Formation in Theological Perspective,* ed. Jeffrey P. Greenman and George Kalantzis (Downers Grove, IL: IVP Academic, 2010), 144.

      treated not as a text to be dissected: Benner, *Opening to God*, 48.

116   *it manifests God's power*: Origen, *Homilies on Joshua* 20.1, ed. Cynthia Whiter and trans. Barbara J. Bruce, Fathers of the Church (Washington, DC: Catholic University of America Press, 2002), 173-76.

      In lectio we read and listen: Hall, "Reading Christ into the Heart," 144.

117   *Mulholland distinguishes famously between*: M. Robert Mulholland Jr., *Invitation to a Journey: A Road Map for Spiritual Formation* (Downers Grove, IL: InterVarsity Press, 1993), 47-60.

      approach Scripture in humility: M. Robert Mulholland Jr., *Shaped by the Word: The Power of Scripture in Spiritual Formation* (Nashville: Upper Room, 1985), 54.

      When we are reluctant to face: Hall, "Reading Christ into the Heart," 149.

121   *David's emphasis is on listening*: Constance M. Cherry, *The Worship Architect: A Blueprint for Designing Culturally Relevant and Biblically Faithful Services* (Grand Rapids, MI: Baker Academic, 2010), 70.

124   *Eugene Peterson challenges the church*: Peterson, *Eat This Book* (Grand Rapids, MI: Eerdmans, 2006), loc. 209, Kindle.

8 CORPORATE CONFESSION: THE GIFT
OF AN UNFETTERED CONSCIENCE

126   *The majority of confessions in Scripture*: Patrick D. Miller, *They Cried to the Lord: The Form and Theology of Biblical Prayer* (Minneapolis: Fortress Press, 1994), 250.

Even when occurring privately: Patrick Miller also notes that Joshua confronting Achan about stealing forbidden valuables from Jericho as well as Ezra's prayers of repentance recorded in Ezra 9 and Nehemiah 9 are all set in the context of a public assembly. See Miller, *They Cried to the Lord*, 250-51.

I (or we) have sinned: See Exodus 9:27; Numbers 22:34; Judges 10:15; 1 Samuel 12:10; 15:30; 2 Samuel 19:20; 24:10; 1 Kings 8:47; Psalm 106:6; Daniel 9:5; Nehemiah 1:6.

127   *I (or we) have sinned against the Lord*: Exodus 10:16; Deuteronomy 1:41; Judges 10:10; 1 Samuel 7:6; 2 Samuel 12:13; Psalm 41:4; 51:4; Jeremiah 14:7, 20; Nehemiah 1:6.

128   *Scripture invites us to consider*: Grant R. Osborne, *James, 1-2 Peter, Jude*, Cornerstone Biblical Commentary 18 (Carol Stream, IL: Tyndale House, 2011), 119.

Christians have an urgent and continual: Miller, *They Cried to the Lord*, 260.

confess their failings publicly: Didache 4.14.

the framers of the Didache *trusted*: Aaron Milavec, *The Didache: Text, Translation, Analysis and Commentary* (Collegeville, MN: Liturgical Press, 2003), 61.

Hughes Oliphant Old explains the exclusion: Hughes Oliphant Old, *Leading in Prayer: A Workbook for Worship* (Grand Rapids, MI: Eerdmans, 1995), 80.

Miller adds that the early church's: Miller, *They Cried to the Lord*, 260.

The Middle Ages witnessed: Old, *Leading in Prayer*, 80.

129   *Reformers crafted new prayers*: Old, *Leading in Prayer*, 81.

restoring the practice of public confession: Michael Horton, *A Better Way: Rediscovering the Drama of Christ-Centered Worship* (Grand Rapids, MI: Baker Books, 2002), 152.

As we become more spiritually attuned: Ruth Haley Barton, *Sacred Rhythms: Arranging Our Lives for Spiritual Transformation* (Downers Grove, IL: InterVarsity Press, 2006), 92.

130   *self-examination awakens us to the presence*: Barton, *Sacred Rhythms*, 93.

a warp in the divine order: Miller, *They Cried to the Lord*, 248.

130   *After convicting us of sin*: Miller, *They Cried to the Lord*, 248.

      Confession invites us to say: Barton, *Sacred Rhythms*, 103.

133   *self-examination, rightly practiced*: Barton, *Sacred Rhythms*, 93.

      Augustine worked through this psalm: Augustine, *Exposition of the Psalms*, trans.
      Maria Boulding, Works of Saint Augustine 25.3 (Hyde Park, NY: New City
      Press, 2000), 254.

134   *Dietrich Bonhoeffer teaches*: Dietrich Bonhoeffer, *Life Together* (New York: Harper-
      Collins, 1954), 110.

      where there's inauthentic community: Bonhoeffer, *Life Together*, 110.

      one who is alone with their sin: Bonhoeffer, *Life Together*, 110.

135   *The church's prayer of confession*: Mark Labberton, *The Dangerous Act of Worship:
      Living God's Call to Justice* (Downers Grove, IL: InterVarsity Press, 2007), 117.

      corporate repentance culminates with: Constance M. Cherry, *The Worship Architect:
      A Blueprint for Designing Culturally Relevant and Biblically Faithful Services*
      (Grand Rapids, MI: Baker Academic, 2010), 148.

      absolution assures worshipers: Cherry, *Worship Architect*, 143.

136   *Curt Thompson insightfully observes*: Curt Thompson, *Anatomy of the Soul: Sur-
      prising Connections Between Neuroscience and Spiritual Practices That Can
      Transform Your Life and Relationships* (Carol Stream, IL: Tyndale House, 2010),
      230.

      divine forgiveness fills the room: Thompson, *Anatomy of the Soul*, 230.

139   *God begins the process*: All attempts to locate the source of this prayer have proven
      unsuccessful. If you can provide source information, please email it to rory
      @heartoftheartist.org.

140   *Regarding what words to use*: Hughes Oliphant Old, for example, offers a wonderful
      collection of confessional prayers for worship all based on Scripture. See Old,
      Leading in Prayer, 85-137.

      We confess that we have sinned: See *Evangelical Lutheran Worship* (Minneapolis:
      Augsburg Fortress, 2006), 95; and *The Book of Common Prayer* (New York:
      Oxford University Press, 1990), 360.

141   *a delightful exchange between*: Hoyt L. Hickman, Don E. Saliers, Laurence Hull
      Stookey, and James F. White, *The New Handbook of the Christian Year* (Nash-
      ville: Abingdon Press, 1992), 123.

      After confession in many Lutheran churches: *Evangelical Lutheran Worship*, 96.

9 Lord's Supper as Spiritual Nourishment

143 *According to Justin Martyr*: Justin Martyr, *First Apology* 66.2, ed. and trans. Edward Rochie Hardy, Early Christian Fathers (New York: Macmillan, 1970), 286.

The pioneers of our faith: Edward Foley, *From Age to Age: How Christians Have Celebrated the Eucharist* (Collegeville, MN: Liturgical Press, 2008), 76.

fulfilling their baptismal commitment: John H. McKenna, *Become What You Receive: A Systematic Study of the Eucharist* (Mundelein, IL: Hillenbrand Books, 2012), 145.

the salvation of our soul and body: Thomas à Kempis, *The Imitation of Christ: In Four Books*, ed. and trans. Joseph N. Tylenda (New York: Vintage Books, 1998), 4.4.

When the bread is given: John Calvin, *Institutes of the Christian Religion* 4.17.3, ed. John T. McNeill, trans. Ford Lewis Battles (Philadelphia: Westminster Press, 1960).

144 *The phrase in remembrance*: Gordon T. Smith, *A Holy Meal: The Lord's Supper in the Life of the Church* (Grand Rapids, MI: Baker Academic, 2005), 39.

145 *Emmaus illustrates how Jesus' disciples*: Joseph A. Fitzmyer, *The Gospel According to Luke X-XXIV*, Anchor Bible (Garden City, NY: Doubleday, 1985), 1559.

Brant Pitre suggests: Brant Pitre, *Jesus and the Jewish Roots of the Eucharist: Unlocking the Secrets of the Last Supper* (New York: Image, 2016), 201.

Justin Martyr states: Justin Martyr, *First Apology* 66.2, 286.

146 *New Testament church was not concerned*: Kenneth Leech, *Experiencing God: Theology as Spirituality* (Eugene: Wipf & Stock, 2002), 281.

All attempts to explain: Leonard J. Vander Zee, *Christ, Baptism and the Lord's Supper: Recovering the Sacraments for Evangelical Worship* (Downers Grove, IL: InterVarsity Press, 2004), 200.

John Calvin asserts: Calvin, *Institutes* 4.17.3.

Christians are invited to come: David A. deSilva, *Sacramental Life: Spiritual Formation Through the Book of Common Prayer* (Downers Grove, IL: InterVarsity Press, 2008), 85.

We are to approach Communion: Leech, *Experiencing God*, 265.

147 *Everything Jesus offered his first disciples*: Patrick Malloy, *Celebrating the Eucharist: A Practical Guide for Clergy and Other Liturgical Ministers* (New York: Church Publishing, 2007), loc. 1607, Kindle.

148 *the eucharistic sacrifice is a microcosm*: Leech, *Experiencing God*, 280-81.

The word translated "participation": Joseph A. Fitzmyer, *First Corinthians: A New Translation with Introduction and Commentary*, Anchor Yale Bible 32 (New Haven, CT: Yale University Press, 2008), 390.

148   *diverse people joining together*: Richard A. Horsley, *1 Corinthians,* Abingdon New
       Testament Commentaries (Nashville: Abingdon Press, 1998), 158.

       they were anything but together: Horsley, *1 Corinthians,* 158.

149   *Leonard Vander Zee rightly concludes*: Vander Zee, *Christ, Baptism and the Lord's
       Supper,* 157.

       The bond of friendship enjoyed: Alasdair I. C. Heron, *Table and Tradition: Toward an
       Ecumenical Understanding of the Eucharist* (Philadelphia: Westminster Press,
       1983), 25.

       The first-century Greco-Roman: Patrick T. McCormick, *A Banqueter's Guide to the
       All-Night Soup Kitchen of the Kingdom of God* (Collegeville, MN: Liturgical
       Press, 2004), 52.

       we become that which we receive: Bernard P. Prusak, "Explaining Eucharistic 'Real
       Presence': Moving beyond a Medieval Conundrum," *Theological Studies* 75, no.
       2 (June 2014): 256.

150   *the* Didache *required churchgoers*: *Didache* 14.2.

       John Calvin warned his congregants: Elsie Anne McKee, ed., *John Calvin: Writings on
       Pastoral Piety* (New York: Paulist Press, 2001), 108.

       The forgiveness believers experience: Smith, *Holy Meal,* 65-66.

       Communion necessitates reconciliation: James K. A. Smith, *Desiring the Kingdom:
       Worship, Worldview, and Cultural Formation* (Grand Rapids, MI: Baker Aca-
       demic, 2009), 202.

       Alexander Schmemann adds: Alexander Schmemann, *For the Life of the World*
       (Crestwood, NY: St. Vladimir's Seminary Press, 2004), 45.

151   *Gaius's house held forty to sixty people*: John Mark Hicks, *Come to the Table: Revi-
       sioning the Lord's Supper* (Abilene, TX: Leafwood, 2002), 116.

       preferential treatment to rich people: Hicks, *Come to the Table,* 116.

       Wealthy members likely arrived early: Raymond F. Collins, *First Corinthians,* Sacra
       Pagina 7 (Collegeville, MN: Michael Glazier, 1999), 418.

152   *first-century Mediterranean banquets*: Horsley, *1 Corinthians,* 160; and Collins, *First
       Corinthians,* 418.

       slaves and day laborers: Collins, *First Corinthians,* 418.

       Arriving later, slaves and manual laborers: Collins, *First Corinthians,* 418-19.

       the Eucharist became a divisive event: Hicks, *Come to the Table,* 115-16.

153   *the Eucharist as a "converting ordinance"*: For example, John Wesley, cited in Gordon
       T. Smith, *A Holy Meal: The Lord's Supper in the Life of the Church* (Grand Rapids,

MI: Baker Academic, 2005), 78; Timothy Keller, "Evangelistic Worship," *Gospel in Life.com*, accessed June 28, 2018, 7, https://static1.squarespace.com /static/5315f2e5e4b04a00bc148f24/t/537a726be4b0d45559686db1 /1400533611277/Evangelistic_Worship.pdf); and Leonard Vander Zee, *Christ, Baptism and the Lord's Supper: Recovering the Sacraments for Evangelical Worship* (Downers Grove, IL: IVP Academic, 2004), 137.

154   *The Eucharist brings to mind*: McCormick, *Banqueter's Guide*, 26.

  Those who are well-off: Justin Martyr, *Apology on Behalf of Christians* 67.6-7, in *Justin, Philosopher and Martyr: Apologies*, ed. Denis Minns and Paul Parvis, Oxford Early Christian Texts (New York: Oxford University Press, 2009), 261.

155   *If participation in the Lord's Supper*: Smith, *Holy Meal*, 74.

156   *The bread!*: Lewis B. Smedes, *All Things Made New: A Theology of Man's Union with Christ* (Grand Rapids, MI: Eerdmans, 1970), 239.

  weekly observances had become the norm: Robert F. Taft, *Beyond East and West: Problems in Liturgical Understanding* (Rome: Pontifical Oriental Institute, 2011), 88.

157   *Eucharist less frequently than once a week*: Taft, *Beyond East and West*, 109.

159   *bread doesn't come from a single grain*: Augustine of Hippo, *Homily 272*, www.early churchtexts.com/public/augustine_sermon_272_eucharist.htm, 2. See also *Didache* 8.4.

  Jesus insistence that our eating: Other pertinent Scripture passages include Luke 22:30; Revelation 21:2, 9; 22:17.

  the party to end all parties: Zac Hicks, *The Worship Pastor: A Call to Ministry for Worship Leaders and Teams* (Grand Rapids, MI: Zondervan, 2016), 139.

  Constance Cherry likens the Table: Constance M. Cherry, *The Worship Architect: A Blueprint for Designing Culturally Relevant and Biblically Faithful Services* (Grand Rapids, MI: Baker Academic, 2010), 89.

160   *an always-new and ever-flowing*: Sister Heidi, "The Celebration of the Eucharist: Some Consequences for the Formation of the Religious Life," *Ecumenical Review* 38, no. 3 (July 1986): 295-96.

10 Living in Our Baptism

162   *"The Two Ways"*: *Didache* 1.1.

  the Didache *stipulated*: Aaron Milavec, *The Didache: Text, Translation, Analysis and Commentary* (Collegeville, MN: Liturgical Press, 2003), 64.

163   *Even after their baptism*: Laurence Hull Stookey, *Baptism: Christ's Act in the Church* (Nashville: Abingdon Press, 1982), 104-5.

163   *Egeria describes the bishop*: Egeria, *Itinerarium Egeriae* 46.1, in *The Pilgrimage of Egeria*, trans. Anne McGowan and Paul F. Bradshaw (Collegeville, MN: Liturgical Press Academic, 2018), 189-90.

164   *renouncing Satan and all his ways*: Cyril, *Mystagogical Catechesis* 1.4, in *St. Cyril of Jerusalem's Lectures on the Christian Sacraments: The Procatechesis and the Five Mystagogical Catecheses*, ed. F. L. Cross (Crestwood, NY: St. Vladimir's Seminary Press, 1995).

       encouraging believers to remember their baptism: Martin Luther, *The Large Catechism*, trans. Robert H. Fischer (Philadelphia: Fortress Press, 1959), 83, 85-86.

165   *lives of faithful obedience*: Leonard J. Vander Zee, *Christ, Baptism and the Lord's Supper: Recovering the Sacraments for Evangelical Worship* (Downers Grove, IL: InterVarsity Press, 2004), 92.

       John Calvin insists: John Calvin, *Institutes* 4.15.3.

166   *Calvin encourages believers to remember*: Calvin, *Institutes* 4.15.3.

       Though we often return: Vander Zee, *Christ, Baptism and the Lord's Supper*, 117.

       correct to say that Baptism: Martin Luther, "The Babylonian Captivity of the Church," in *Luther's Works: Word and Sacrament 2*, ed. Abdel Ross Wentz (Philadelphia: Muhlenberg, 1959), 36:68.

167   *Those united with Christ in baptism*: David A. deSilva, *Sacramental Life: Spiritual Formation Through the Book of Common Prayer* (Downers Grove, IL: InterVarsity Press, 2008), 33.

168   *heavens were forcefully torn open*: Vander Zee, *Christ, Baptism and the Lord's Supper*, 82.

169   *we become as pleasing*: Frederick Dale Bruner, *The Christbook: A Historical/Theological Commentary, Matthew 1-12* (Waco, TX: Word, 1987), 92.

       Throughout the New Testament: See, for example, 1 Corinthians 6:11; 12:13; Titus 3:5.

       baptism obligates God: Vander Zee, *Christ, Baptism and the Lord's Supper*, 94-95.

170   *Holy Spirit accomplishes in us*: Vander Zee, *Christ, Baptism and the Lord's Supper*, 94.

       you don't need additional, supernatural experience: Bruner bluntly takes to task those who espouse a "baptism of the Spirit" apart from baptism: "The Pentecostals and Charismatics are wrong in offering a Baptism in the Spirit independent of and even superior to Baptism 'into the name of the Father and of the Son and of the Holy Spirit.'" See Bruner, *Christbook*, 80.

172   *Great indeed is the Baptism*: Cyril, *Procatechesis* 16, in Cross, *St. Cyril of Jerusalem's Lectures on the Christian Sacraments*.

173   *questions from the Book of Common Prayer*: *The Book of Common Prayer and Administration of the Sacraments and Other Rites and Ceremonies of the Church* (New York: Oxford University Press, 1990), 302-3.

EPILOGUE: WE GET TO DO THIS!

176   *see the glory of the Lord:* Michael J. Gorman, *Participating in Christ: Explorations in Paul's Theology and Spirituality* (Grand Rapids, MI: Baker Academic, 2019), 216-17.

APPENDIX 1: RESPONSIVE SCRIPTURE READING

177   *The following reading:* Melanie Ross, *Evangelical Versus Liturgical? Defying a Dichotomy* (Grand Rapids, MI: Eerdmans, 2014), 105-6.

APPENDIX 3: CORPORATE PRAYER OF CONFESSION

182   *Corporate Prayer of Confession*: *The Book of Common Worship* (Louisville: Westminster John Knox, 1993), 404-6.

TRANSFORMING CENTER®

Strengthen The Soul Of Your Leadership

Don't just learn about spiritual transformation— experience it in your own life and leadership!

The Transforming Center exists to strengthen the souls of pastors, Christian leaders, and the congregations and organizations they serve. The best thing you bring to leadership is your own transforming self!

Visit the Transforming Center online to learn more about:

- *Transforming Community*®: A two-year experience of spiritual formation for leaders
- Earning a doctor of ministry, a master's specialization or a certificate in spiritual transformation
- The *Strengthening the Soul of Your Leadership* podcast
- Teaching and transformational experiences for your congregation
- *Transforming Church*®: A network of churches and leaders who affirm that spiritual transformation is central to the Gospel and therefore central to the mission of the church
- *Transforming Resources*®: Print and electronic tools to guide leaders and their communities in experiencing spiritual transformation

Join thousands of pastors and Christian leaders . . .

receive *Beyond Words*®, reflections on the soul of leadership.

To subscribe, visit:
www.TransformingCenter.org

TRANSFORMING | Resources®

Tools to guide leaders and their communities in experiencing spiritual transformation.

Beyond mere information, each resource is designed to provide step-by-step guidance for engaging the practices, experiences and relationships that foster greater intimacy with God and deeper levels of spiritual transformation.

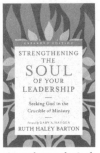

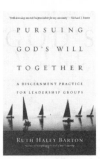

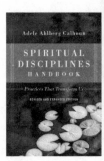

Strengthening the Soul
of Your Leadership

Life Together in Christ

Pursuing God's
Will Together

Spiritual Disciplines
Handbook, Revised

Sacred Rhythms

Sacred Rhythms DVD
curriculum

Invitation to Solitude
and Silence

Invitation to Retreat

Invitations from God

To see the complete library of Transforming Resources, visit:
www.Resources.TransformingCenter.org